Crack Climbing!

HOW TO CLIMB™ SERIES

Crack Climbing!

Lisa Gnade

and

Steve Petro

GUILFORD, CONNECTICUT
HELENA, MONTANA
AN IMPRINT OF THE GLOBE PEQUOT PRESS

FALCONGUIDES®

"Have I Left the Eagle to Soar in Freedom" is reprinted from *The Best of Chief Dan George,* by Chief Dan George and Helmut Hirnschall. Used by permission from Hancock House Publishers (www.hancockhouse.com).

Interior photos are by Lisa Gnade and Steve Petro unless noted otherwise.

Text design by Casey Shain
Illustrations by Lisa Gnade

Library of Congress Cataloging-in-Publication Data
Gnade, Lisa.
 Crack Climbing! / Lisa Gnade, Steve Petro.
   p. cm. —(How to climb?)
 ISBN 978-0-7627-4591-3
   1. Free climbing. I. Petro, Steve. II. Title.
 GV200.25.G63 2008
 796.522'3—dc22

                                                2008011162

Printed in China
10 9 8 7 6 5 4 3 2 1

Hanging out in the Crack House, Utah.

Contents

PART II: *Equipment*

PART III: *Hitting the Crags*

Acknowledgments

We'd like to extend huge and special thanks to Brian Bailey for the use of his vivid and inspirational photography in this book. His images capture the spirit of crack climbing and the beauty of the areas in which they were taken. We'd go so far as to state that no book on crack climbing would be complete without his photos. Brian Bailey, aka King, is an amazing, gifted photographer—and above that, he's loads of fun to share a rope, a photo session, and a campfire with!

Big thanks also go to photographers Dawn Kish, Simon Carter, Sebastian Schwertner, Uli Lenk, and Red Chili/Klaus Fengler for allowing us to use their images.

Over the years we've had the great fortune of climbing with countless partners across the globe. We've enjoyed learning with and from each of them. A great day at the crags isn't just about the routes, it's also about the people. A beautiful place, a stunning line, and good friends to experience it with—for us, that's the joie de vivre!

Lisa Grade

Steve Petro

Introduction

We have a special love for crack climbing. Although we have successfully climbed sport routes in twelve countries at difficulty grades equaling those of our hardest crack achievements, we rarely pass up the opportunity to climb a stunning crack of any grade. We consider our successes on certain cracks among our most memorable and rewarding climbing accomplishments. Some of our favorites are tremendously difficult; some are simply a lot of fun. Others must be done a hundred times for the sheer joy of it!

Both of us had our first climbing experiences on cracks. For years after that we climbed cracks almost exclusively. One of Lisa's most significant turning points as a climber was when she saw a photo of Indian Creek's *Tricks Are for Kids* and knew that it was not a question of *if* she would climb it, but *when*. Steve's romance with cracks started as a choice between cracks and slabs. Say no more!

It may be the fun and fluid motion of crack climbing, the sustained athleticism required, the "head" for placing gear, or even the amazing like-minded individuals we meet at the crags that attract us to this sport. But more than all that, we like clipping the anchor on a wonderfully strenuous crack and experiencing the worn-out yet satisfied feeling of arriving home at the end of a long, happy journey. There's no place like home!

Lisa Gnade stemming on Mr. Clean (5.11a), Devil's Tower. SIMON CARTER

Our Mission

Our goal in this book is to empower and compel you to climb cracks by answering those common initial questions: *How?* and *Why?* In so doing, we hope you'll come to better understand and appreciate this sport. Understanding leads to confidence,

Climbing isn't just about the routes; it's also about good friends and fun days at the crag.

which in turn empowers. As in life, so in crack climbing: Preparedness enables opportunity. Of course no book is a substitute for real-life experience, but we do hope to provide you with a blueprint from which to build your dreams and plans for this new endeavor.

This book is designed as a comprehensive overview of crack climbing, including an introductory section on different rock types and the unique qualities of the cracks that form in each. Following that, part I offers complete descriptions of jamming and other crack climbing techniques, accompanied by illustrations and photos; part II covers the art of protection and other equipment considerations; and part III offers practical suggestions for hitting the crags, including where to go, what to climb, and how to start leading in the safest manner possible. Throughout, we'll expose you to terminology specific to crack climbing; these terms are all rounded up in the glossary at the end of the book.

Note: We've assumed that you already understand basic safety concepts such as tying a proper knot and belaying, as well as other roped climbing fundamentals. If you don't, consult John Long's *How to Rock Climb!*

Rocks and Cracks

Cracks are formed in numerous rock types, in a variety of ways. Water erosion can form or widen existing cracks and seams in rock. Sometimes cracks are human-made, via explosions. Other times, tiny seams are made wide enough for crack climbing by years of aid climbing; we'll discuss this more later in the book.

Let's take a look at a few of the best rock types for crack climbing at a smattering of well-known areas.

Some cracks form when igneous rock such as **basalt** or **phonolite porphyry** cools. As molten rock cools, it sometimes forms columns; these contract with solidification, leaving cracks between them. The cracks in turn lend themselves to some of the best crack climbing around. Good examples include Paradise Forks in northern Arizona and Devils Tower in Wyoming.

As basalt cools, it contracts and forms columns that are jointed, like tightly packed pencils. Basalt columns are typically six-sided but may also form in four-, five-, or seven-sided pillars.

The **basalt** at Paradise Forks is a skin-friendly, fine-grained, dark-colored rock that is very hard and resistant to weathering. It is volcanic in origin, having flowed from vents at temperatures between 2,000 and 2,300 degrees F. It cooled so rapidly on the earth's surface that individual crystals did not have time to grow large enough to be seen with the naked eye. As it cooled, it contracted and formed columns that are jointed like tightly packed pencils. These columns are typically six-sided, but basalt may also form four-, five-, or seven-sided pillars.

The 1,253-foot stump of phonolite porphyry at Devils Tower formed about fifty million years ago when liquid hot magma forced its way up between layers of sedimentary rock. It probably cooled at a shallow level—perhaps 700 feet below the surface. As it cooled, it shrank and fractured to form mostly five-sided, jointed columns. Current research suggests that Devils Tower is not the remnant of an extinct volcano as previously thought, but rather a laccolith (like a pimple of magma) that welled up between preexisting rock layers.

Setting a fist jam in Yosemite granite. DAWN KISH

Yosemite's **granite** is the most famous granite for rock climbing in the world. A hundred thirty million years in the making, the Sierra Nevada batholithic (the term comes from the Greek: *bathos* means "deep," while *lithos* is "rock") complex comprises hundreds of individual plutons (named for Pluto, the Roman god of the underworld) of rock. The region's geology is so fascinating that it has been the subject of many books and innumerable research papers.

Approximately 103 million years ago, the plu-ton of granite that formed the Yosemite landmarks El Capitan and Cathedral Spires forced its way through an older pluton. This is only one example of the Valley's various plutonic intrusions. Yosemite's Leaning Tower is an example of another granitic-type pluton called **granodiorite,** having character-istic dark, rounded mineral clots.

Eighty million years have passed since these batholithic plutons first crystallized, cooled, uplifted, and eroded. Glaciers have come and gone, scouring the Valley's walls. The continual process of geologi-

Prime crack climbing in Indian Creek occurs on the early-Jurassic Wingate Sandstone.

cal change has built Yosemite's beloved superstructures, the crack-bearing cliffs we climb today.

Sandstone, as seen on the miles of cliffs in Indian Creek Canyon near Canyonlands National Park, Utah, is a sedimentary rock. The prime climbing in Indian Creek occurs on the early-Jurassic Wingate Sandstone.

Wingate is hard, reddish brown, fine-grained, and well-sorted sandstone. It's an aeolian, or wind deposit, that was laid down atop earlier layers of different sandstones. Wingate was deposited around 200 million years ago when southern Utah was dry and covered by a vast desert of sand dunes. As the dunes migrated, they formed huge cross-bedded layers. Over time the Wingate layer was covered by other sandstones and buried. The cliffs formed their

renowned cracks when an uplift affected the plateau, forcing layers of rock to rise; then time, erosion, gravity, and settling caused splitting of the individual layers.

Cracks and Us

At first sight the naturally occurring lines of many cracks provide visual inspiration. Many cracks seemingly beg to be climbed. Some lines are obvious. Others appear graceful, powerful, impossible, or frightful. Some can be tricky or even nasty. In those situations it helps to keep telling yourself that cracks are fun.

Motivation for crack climbing is a personal matter. The reasons for undertaking any sport are unique to the individual athlete. There is no single, universal explanation for crack climbing's appeal. Answers to the question *Why?* may range from the whimsical "To get to the top!" to deeply philosophical reflections on your fondness for placing gear, your tendency toward sadomasochism, or even the well-rehearsed old shtick about enjoying a good challenge.

You'll hear accusations like "You're crazy," "You're a real daredevil," or "You're irresponsible" from a largely uninformed public—many members of whom, sadly, are unwilling to leave the couch for anything as demanding as a hands-on experience. Cover your ears! This negativity could be self-justification—a way of belittling other people's hard work to further their own inaction. Besides, what's more dangerous and irresponsible: engaging in a sport that's protected by high-tech safety equipment and that challenges body and mind, or mentally and physically vegetating while wolfing down high-fat foods in front of a radiation-emitting screen? Crack climbing is an exhilarating, all-body-working, confidence-building labor.

No doubt about it: Gazing up from the base of a 160-foot line with a rack heavy with gear and a mind full of questions can be a daunting experience. Endeavor to persevere! The rewards for accepting the challenge are many. Exercising your ability to bravely go beyond and overcome an obstacle that once loomed as impossible is fortifying for both mind and body. And when it's not, remember to tell yourself that cracks are fun.

Despite human projections onto a rock, cracks demand a knowledge base distinct from other types of climbing (such as sport climbing and bouldering). Most crack routes demand a new repertoire of techniques, specialized equipment, and safety considerations. That's why we wrote this book.

> *Our ways are good, but only in our world.*
> —CHIEF DAN GEORGE (1899–1981),
> *"WORDS TO A GRANDCHILD"*

Zion National Park has some of the country's finest big-wall crack routes. KLAUS FENGLER/RED CHILI

Rock climbing? You must be crazy!

Getting Started

Back in the day, would-be climbers were largely at the mercy of their own ignorance when learning to climb. An old quadratic bit of wisdom comes to mind:

- There are things you know you know.
- There are things you know you don't know.
- There are things you don't know you don't know.
- There are things you don't know that you actually *do* know.

In climbing the most fun is usually to be had when you know what you know. That said, climbers are often delighted to discover that they know something they'd thought was unknown. Climbing gyms, professional guides, credible mentors, and how-to books can help you learn the things you truly don't know.

Climbing gyms and walls are great places to experience the general concept and movement of climbing. In the last couple of decades, hundreds have sprouted up nationwide. Many of them

Guides or credible mentors can help create a safe climbing experience outdoors on real rock.

Many gyms, like Momentum Indoor Climbing in Sandy, Utah, have incorporated crack features in their architecture.

Katie Griffith learns to crack climb on toprope. Her palm is down for balance while she looks for a hold.

Making a plan from the ground before climbing is key to success and provides a good opportunity for posing it out big-time! BRIAN BAILEY

incorporate crack features in their architecture. The cracks in gyms can vary from extremely realistic shapes and textures quite close to actual rock, to rough approximations made of sanded wood. Either way, they provide an opportunity to learn and practice basic techniques. Most climbing gyms have enthusiastic employees available to give lessons. Some offer courses specific to learning desired skills.

Professional guide services are available in many locations. Guides can create a safe environment in which to experience crack climbing outdoors, on real rock. Although such professional services don't come cheap, they are a good value. Guides provide all or most of the gear, ropes, and other equipment needed for the day; if you request it, they can instruct you on movement techniques. If you're still not entirely confident in your level of preparedness, or you're sitting on the fence when it comes to purchasing your own rack, a guide can be a helpful intermediary.

To find a climbing gym or a rock climbing guide service, consult the phone directory, the Internet, the back of a climbing magazine, or your local retailer of climbing equipment.

Another important point to remember when starting out is that topropes (TRs) offer a low-stress and relatively safe way to learn and apply crack climbing's special techniques. By setting up a TR, you can focus on body kinetics rather than gear placement. Placing gear, of course, is integral to crack climbing and will be discussed later in the book, but a good, safe introduction to the art is available simply by following a leader on a crack and removing the gear. Consider this one step up in difficulty from a regular toprope. Seconding a climb gives you an up-close view of (hopefully) proper placements, and also some idea of the extra energy required to hang out and tangle with gear.

Make a Plan

Let's say that the belay is on and you're tied in and ready to leave the ground on a toprope. What happens now?

Making a plan and paying attention to details are two of the many steps to success. That said, although you can make a visual plan of attack from the ground, climbing an unknown route requires flexibility of thought, reaction to unexpected challenges, and frequent improvisation. Make a plan anyway.

From the ground you can often view the crack's size as well as the overall direction of the route. Anticipating the size of the crack allows you to select the appropriate rack and quickly review and visualize the techniques you'll use. Knowing proven techniques for the particular crack size can turn a cheese-grater nightmare into a methodical breeze.

There is not always one correct solution to a given challenge. Our goal is to equip you with an array of options. We hope you'll practice many of the techniques described in this book, learning for yourself how to select the right tool for the job.

PART I

Crack Climbing Techniques

1

Jamming

To jam is the verb used to describe what you do to ascend a crack. This technique involves fitting your hands, fingers, legs, feet, head, or whole body—or a combination of these parts—into a rock crevice. You wedge the size-appropriate body parts into the crack to create opposing pressure between your skeletal system and the rock.

Hand Jam

A good hand jam can be a climber's best friend. Hand jams also offer a high probability of success for a crack climbing novice, if done correctly. We will discuss the technique at length, since it's an absolute staple for a crack climber's knowledge base. It's like learning to walk before attempting to run and jump.

If a crack is wide enough to accept your hand with contact on both the palm side and the back of the hand at the same time, it's a hand crack. Hand jams can be tight or loose relative to both the size of the crack and the size of the hand.

It's a good idea to look at the crack and find a target for a hand jam. It may be a wider spot in the crack that allows your hand to fit within, or it may be a narrower, constricting spot small enough to hold your hand's skeletal structure when you catch on. Some cracks are parallel-sided, which greatly simplifies the placement selection process.

Once you've selected a target, take time to accurately place your hand there. Accuracy can

Classic hand and foot jams abound in sandstone cracks like this.

Hand jamming is an absolute staple for a crack climber's knowledge base.

alleviate slipping, cutting, excessive energy and time expenditure, emotional pandemonium, and discomfort. Accuracy is a good thing.

The hand may be placed thumbs-up or thumbs-down. (*Thumbs* is often substituted for *thumb* in climber-speak.) Once your hand is in the desired position, cup it, pulling your thumb inward toward the index finger or palm via muscular contraction, and then torque the hand to apply enough outward force against the rock to hold some per-

3

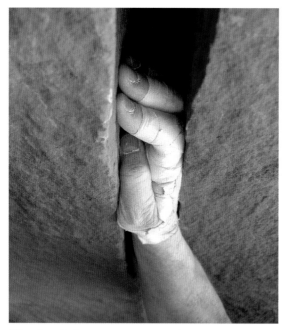

The thumb faces up or outward in a thumbs-up jam.

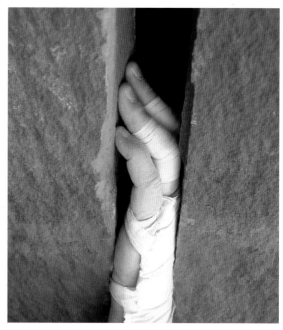

The thumb faces down or inward in a thumbs-down jam.

Sometimes both hands face thumbs-up.
DAWN KISH

Some cracks are jammed with both hands thumbs-down, like this section on Six Star Crack (5.13b).
BRIAN BAILEY

centage (the amount varies with the situation) of your weight. Typically, your other hand and feet are also bearing some of the weight. Ideally, whenever you're moving one hand or one foot, the other appendages form three points of contact with the rock.

Hands may be jammed with both thumbs up, both thumbs down, or a combination of one up and one down. This will depend on the shape and angle of the crack and your own body position.

For example, if you're reaching high overhead, it's usually easiest and feels most secure to get a thumbs-down jam. Frequently, such a jam will allow you to initiate a move from a lower body position if you fully extend your reaching arm and the corresponding side of your torso. Given the way we're jointed, this is typically the most effective position from which to pull, and pull, and pull until your other hand can let go and move above to its own jam.

If you need a very long reach, commonly it's best to have your lower hand jammed in the thumbs-up position. Anatomically speaking, you can almost always move farther upward off a thumbs-up jam than a thumbs-down jam.

When you've just pulled a move from a thumbs-up jam on your right hand to a thumbs-down jam on your left, you're positioned so that your thumbs are pointed toward each other within the crack. If you place your right hand below the left, keeping the right in the thumbs-up orientation, then move your left up again to another thumbs-down jam, you're "shuffling" hands and jams.

*Here, the left hand is jammed thumbs-up, allowing the right hand to reach high for a thumbs-down finger stack (**Winner Takes All, 5.13a, Indian Creek**)* BRIAN BAILEY.

On straight-in cracks or splitters, the most efficient jams typically allow you to hang from a nearly straight-armed, skeletal position. To move upward, contract and bend your arms while keeping the hand jam stationary. When in the bent-arm configuration, it's often most secure and efficient to rotate your elbow downward to a locked position, next to the torso. This creates the coveted torque that is required for technical jams. Fatigue often leads to the elbows creeping up and out, like a little bird about to fly.

To launch a hand-jamming career, Yosemite Valley, California, Fremont Canyon, Wyoming, and Paradise Forks, Arizona, all offer prime pickings.

Foot Jam

Foot jams are key when edges and smears on the face next to the crack are unavailable. These reliable jams are easy to learn and very secure. Cracks sized for hands and fists are typically compatible with foot jams. The main idea is to wedge your foot in the crack to give you a leg to stand on.

To achieve a trusty stance, visually pick a target spot in which to slide your foot. Once you've found a size-appropriate target, you're ready to start the move. First, it's crucial to raise your leg, turning the knee outward so that the foot is alongside your opposite leg. Next, point the foot at the intended jam with your big toe aligned vertically upward, piggy-toe-down. Take time to accurately slide your foot inside the crack in the pre-selected niche. The sole of your shoe will be parallel to the sides of the

Both feet are jammed in the crack.

crack as it slips into place. Once your foot is set, rotate your leg to an upright position, with your knee situated vertically above your foot. A camming action between foot and rock will result from this rotation of the leg to up–down alignment. As such, the cammed foot will form a solid peg on which to stand. After spending a modest amount of time programming yourself to foot jam, you'll quickly be on autopilot, walking up cracks like a gerbil on a wheel.

Toe Jam

Having laid the groundwork via the foot jam, you can move along to more advanced maneuvers. The toe jam is carried out much like the foot jam. The primary difference is that only the toe actively jams, not the foot. Other than the amount of bulk in the crack, the toe jam's mechanics are very similar to a foot jam's.

Inherently, the toe jam is more difficult to control. It's more strenuous and less stable; it occasionally pops out of the crack without a moment's notice because there's less in the crack to begin with. A true toe jam, with all your toes inside the crack, is still quite a secure, steady jam. Cracks that fit thin hands usually also fit toes. The thinner the crack, the less toe you'll use.

It's when the crack is very, very narrow that the going gets rough.

Seek pods to use for potential toe placements in thin cracks, such as finger cracks. Pods are small undulations or divots on the edge of the crack. Even a subtle opening can be a great relief when you're climbing pumpy finger or off-finger cracks. Jams in spots like these may be more speculation than craft. Making them work may involve tenacity and imagination. And even when a crack is too thin to accept the tips of your toes, don't panic—there are still a few tricks in the bag. You may just have to dig a little deeper.

If the wee little tip of a toe starts to go in, it may be prudent to imagine the crack as a vertical edge, rather than a thing to jam. Press your toe hard inward, into the wall, into the crack, and rotate your foot and leg as if you're performing a jam. Concentrate on the edge of the crack under your big toe and use it. Some shoe rubber will catch on this edge, both under your toe and on the rand (the external rubber sidewall of the shoe). A combination of pushing, smearing, control against slipping, and pretending will create a well-planted toe, despite appearances. The better you pretend, the better this technique will work. It's like telling yourself, *You're not getting older. You're getting better. Just do it!*

> *I could be bound by a nutshell, yet count myself king of infinite space, would my thinking make it so.*
>
> —PARAPHRASED FROM WILLIAM SHAKESPEARE'S *HAMLET*

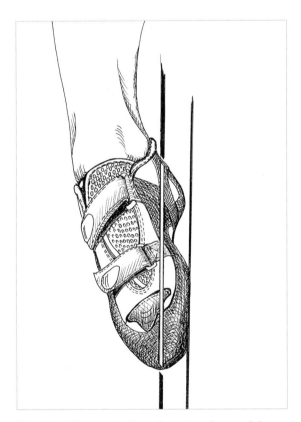

The tip of the toe just barely enters the crack in a thin toe jam.

Thin Hands

Cracks that are too narrow to accept the thickest part of your hand but do accept the knuckles are referred to as thin hands cracks. A solid grasp on hand jamming is crucial to advancing to thin hands. Jamming in thin placements is more strenuous than a sinker hand jam, in which the hand sinks all the way into the crack.

Thin hand jams require you to exert more pressure and usually greater torque on the fingers and front of your hand. More pressure equals harder muscular contraction, hence a faster "pump." (*Pump*? You know . . . that I-can't-make-

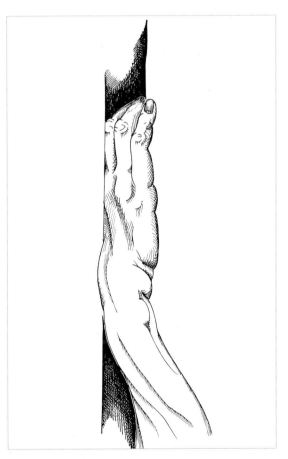

Cracks that are too narrow to accept the thickest part of the hand but do accept the knuckles are referred to as thin hands.

my-fingers-move feeling accompanying the lactic acid burn and cramping from sustained muscular tension.) To create torque, rotate your elbow downward so that it's vertically aligned under your fingers and hand. This joint-twisting action will help create pressure between your skeletal system and the rock, necessary to hold the required amount of body weight.

Thin hand jams can be performed with thumbs up or down, but more often than not thumbs-down provides a more secure jam. It's good to switch between up and down jams to use slightly different muscle groups, giving respite when possible. In either case, it's crucial to push your finger pads against the inside of the crack and squeeze your hand to cause pressure against the inside walls. This will form a camming action between the pads and the finger and hand knuckles. Add sufficient torque and the results are pure magic.

> *Not many people understand what a pump is. It must be experienced to be understood. It is the greatest feeling that I get.*
> —ARNOLD SCHWARZENEGGER

Fingers

Finger jams are mandatory in really thin cracks or spots too thin for hands. These jams come in three main varieties: finger locks, finger jams, and stacks or off-fingers. All finger jams can be performed thumbs-up or -down, per the discussion in the previous "Hand Jam" section. You can accomplish a finger jam using a mono—a single finger—or any number of available fingers and thumbs. Some jams are shallow, permitting only the first digit of the fingertips to enter the crack. Some jams will go two digits deep, while the most popular are sinkers, which go all the way to the joint of the hand. Since we are of the eat-dessert-first mind-set, let's go straight to finger locks.

> *I like monos the best, because the other 9 fingers are resting.*
> —WOLFGANG GÜLLICH (1960–1992)

This climber rests nine fingers while chalking up from a mono finger lock on London Wall, England (E5 6A).

Finger Locks

Finger locks are the stuff of dreams. If you've got an eye for a constriction in a finger-size crack, you'll spot likely places to get a finger lock. The upside of a V-slot marks a natural spot to insert your fingers into the crack. Sliding them in and downward will allow the bones to seat themselves within the crack at the point where the knuckle bones lock into secure contact with the rock. Sometimes there's a slight lip on the crack with the crack becoming gradually wider—we might say it "opens up"—as it recesses inward. Great locks may be as tricky to remove as they were to place. A constricting spot on the lip can provide a textbook example

Steve Petro locks his fingers into place on **Pink Flamingo** *(5.13b), circa 1989.* BRIAN BAILEY

It may be useful to up-slot a finger or hand jam at the base of a downward flare (below a constriction).
DAWN KISH

constriction. This allows you to employ upward force to lock your fingers into a placement. Up-slots are almost always performed thumbs-up, for anatomical reasons.

A classic place to hone finger-locking skills is Devils Tower, Wyoming.

Finger Jams

Standard finger jams are very much like finger locks—just more strenuous. They require more hand contraction and pressure on the crack's walls in order to stay in place. These jams are quite secure and are a staple skill for crack climbing. The

When finger jamming, the fingers torque when the elbows rotate downward to create pressure between bone and crack.

of a finger lock. Here, the joint slots in behind the constriction on the lip as well as into the downward V, creating a win–win situation in which your finger cannot slip out of placement unless you lift your hand.

Finger locks can be relatively relaxing, because they require very little muscular tension and torque to keep the fingers in place. Locked and hanging from the fingers' skeletal system can make a great rest hold to get a shake, catch your breath, and look up the crack to see what's in store. Locks are often ideal jams from which to place gear.

Occasionally, it will be useful to "up-slot" a finger lock or a hand jam in a downward flare below a

basic steps are: You pick a spot that will fit your fingers, accurately articulate your fingers into the crack, and then cam the fingers by rotating your hand. It's usually helpful to rotate your elbow downward. The goal is to create enough outward pressure against the crack to hold the required amount of body weight.

These jams can be done thumbs-up or thumbs-down. Just as in hand jams, it can be useful to vary the orientation of the jams to distribute the strain from specific muscle groups and from the skin and bones themselves to other body parts. Also, depending on your body's balance, the lean of a route, the orientation of a crack in a dihedral, the

Sometimes fingers are jammed while toes edge and smear on the face to maintain balance.

Sometimes a climber will want to jam fingers and toes at the same time.

reach from one hold to another, and a number of other factors, it may be appropriate to choose either an up or down jam.

Inside the crack, your other fingers will usually rest on the lowest one. Many times the thumb is outside the crack, not jammed, pushing against the wall of the crack opposite the finger pads. In other instances, the thumb may push against your forefinger, pull with the finger pads on the same side of the crack, or simply smear against the outside wall.

For a full dose and range of finger jams, plan a trip to Indian Creek, Utah.

Yosemite's granite often requires finger stacks.
DAWN KISH

Finger stacks are performed when cracks are off-finger size, meaning finger jams are rattley but the hand is too big to fit.

Stacks or Off-Fingers

The rattley jams known as stacks or off-fingers are fundamentally the same as the jams described above. In fact, they're just like finger jams, except they're far less secure, require loads of pressure to hold, necessitate greater strength, are very pumpy, can slip out of the crack without warning, hurt quite a bit, can rip skin easily, take more practice to learn than other common jams . . . and are extremely rewarding when effectively executed. Learning to make stacks work is well worth the effort.

You'll use stacks when a crack isn't big enough for your hand to enter, but is too big for a snug-fitting finger jam. Loose jams can make off-fingers-size cracks feel very intimidating. Don't worry. We have ways to make you like it.

Place your fingers inside the crack. Form a stack by putting your middle finger over your forefinger; the ring finger will push hard against the middle. Your pinkie is then crushed between your ring finger and the side of the crack. The thumb will tuck under the forefinger, within the crack, becoming part of the stack of jammed digits. An alternative method has your thumb tucked into the crack and pressed over the nail on your forefinger

Off-finger cracks like **Optimator** *call for finger stacks.* BRIAN BAILEY

Climbing gyms with crack features give climbers the opportunity to learn how to stack before heading to the crag. Here the climber is practicing a ring lock.

Wide hand jams work in cracks that are too roomy for standard, snug-fitting hand jams but too tight for fists.

or even on the nail of your middle finger. Some people call this a "ring lock."

Now the fun begins. Twist the stack and rotate your hand and forearm to a vertical position, keeping your arm close to the wall. Squeeze your hand to tighten the stack and create enough pressure against the rock to hold the necessary percentage of body weight.

Remember, there's no such thing as a bad size. People will ask, "What's your bad size?" Just tell them with conviction there isn't one.

Wide Hands

A wide hand jam works in a crack that's too wide for a standard, snug-fitting hand jam but too tight to fit a fist jam. Wide hand jams are much like hand jams, except your hand must be held in a more deeply cupped shape to fit inside the crack. In wide hand jams contact with the crack is made primarily on the meaty part of your thumb, the outside edge of your forefinger and its hand knuckle, and the pinkie edge of your hand. You must

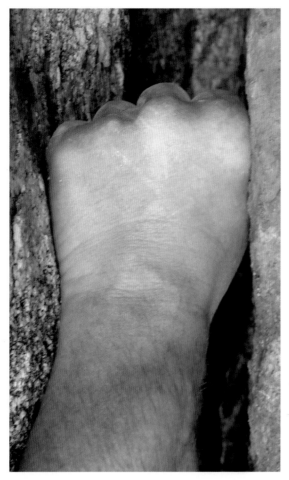

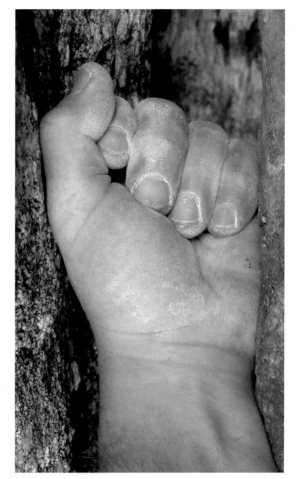

A fist can also be placed with the palm facing down or in.

Fist jams can be formed with the palm facing up or out.

squeeze your hand rigorously to create enough holding pressure against the walls of the crack.

Fist Jam

When a crack is too wide to hold hand jams, it may be conducive to fist jams.

You can perform a fist jam with the palm either facing inward/downward or facing outward/upward. As in hand or finger jams, it may be advantageous to combine the orientation of your fists, and to shuffle the jams. To make a long reach from a jammed fist, it's usually more efficient to move from a palm-out/up placement. When logical, it's good to switch fist orientation on successive moves to preserve energy.

Place your open hand into the crack, then curl your fingers down to make a fist. Your thumb will pull toward your palm and wrap over your first finger or two. You could instead tuck your thumb under the fingers, which increases the fist size, but this can be somewhat painful. The sides of your hand will wedge against the rock. Squeezing turns the fist into a solid chock.

2

Off-Widths and Chimneys

Off-Width Techniques

Off-width is the name given to cracks
that fit neither fist nor torso. Climbing an off-width is more like
wrestling a greased-up Olympian
than performing a ballet. Off-widths
are strenuous. They take tremendous
core strength and a plethora of
moves. They also take a lot of grit
and special outfits. For a crash course
in off-widths, round up the cowboy
hat, long sleeves, and knee pads
and head 'em out to Vedauwoo,
Wyoming!

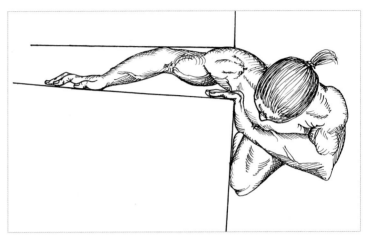

An arm bar often works when a fist jam is too loose.

Arm Bar

There are several variations on the
arm bar. Let's start with one of the thinnest applications for this amazing tool, then work toward larger
sizes.

If a crack is just beyond the hand- or fist-size
range, or flaring so that neither jam is secure
enough to hold your body weight, a combination of
techniques might do the trick.

For example, you could use a loose, deeply
cupped hand jam in conjunction with leverage on
the bones in your forearm. Begin by pushing the
fingertips and the heel of your hand against one
side of the crack. Simultaneously, press the back of
your hand on the opposite side of the crack and

*Todd Smith buries his arm in a Joshua Tree
off-width.*

lever the bones of the forearm on that same side by
bending your wrist until there is weight-bearing
contact.

If the crack is a bit wider than cupped-hand
size, it may be convenient to get a fist jam and then
lever your forearm bones as described above.

For cracks that are wider yet, it may not be
possible to get a hand or a fist to stick. You may
need to use an open hand, palming one side of the
crack while your arm sinks deeper on the forearm
or even beyond the elbow. Your upper forearm or
elbow will then press on the opposite side of the
crack. The wider the crack, the greater the bend in
your elbow.

While one arm is barring, you can use the
other hand to Gaston (reverse side-pull); you can
also cup it around the edge of the crack or place it

Chicken wings and heel–toe jams come in handy when a crack is too wide for an arm bar but the entire torso cannot fit comfortably inside the crack.

just inside the crack. Holding a Gaston on the rim supplies a stabilizing point. This contact will allow you to readjust the arm bar or to move your feet with greater ease. Applying simultaneous sideways and downward force to this hand, in conjunction with pressing on foot jams, will help send your body upward. Feel for edges or undulations deep inside the crack to provide relief from the repetitious arm bar that may cramp your hand or rub all the skin from your elbow.

Chicken Wing

This technique not only has an amusing name, but it's fun to do.

When a classic arm bar has a sloppy, wide fit, but the crack is too narrow to slide your torso inside, it may be time for the chicken wing. The overall action of the chicken wing is like that of a spring-loaded hinge expanding to fill the crack's space.

To try this move, turn sideways to the crack. Then insert and deeply bend the arm nearest the rock with your elbow extended outward, away from your body. Your hand is now by your head or chest. Apply pressure to this hand to palm the inside of the crack while you force the back of your upper arm against the opposite, back side of the crack. Your hand may be close enough to the crack's outside edge that you can wrap the fingers around the arête, giving options for extra friction and multidirectional pulls.

Your other arm and hand will be outside the crack, free for other tasks. You can use this hand to help by wrapping the thumb and fingers around the edge of the crack and pushing out and down, taking some of the strain off your first hand. Your free hand is also available to place gear or scour the face of the wall for handholds such as edges, pockets, slopers (sloping holds), and other textural spots of usefulness.

Feet in an Off-Width

Off-width footwork calls for a number of tactics.

Causing opposing pressure with heel and toe is the entrance exam—the prerequisite to off-width 101. Heel–toe jams are simple to understand and

In a chicken-wing position, the inside arm's elbow is up and points away from the body while the hand palms the rock to the front. The other hand palms the crack's edge while the foot performs a heel–toe jam.

not difficult to do. They come into play when a crack is too wide for a standard foot jam. Begin by inserting your foot into the crack. Twist the ankle so that your toe pushes on one side of the crack and your heel pushes on the other. The other foot can also heel–toe, or you can use it outside the crack on the face, on holds or smears.

If the crack is wide enough, it may be logical to stick your leg inside. This will allow you to use your knee as a chock, a point on which to bar, scum (friction a body part against the rock in an ill-defined kind of way), or jam. Usually the heel and foot oppose the pressure of the knee. Thigh bars and thigh jams work well, too, if crack size permits. All of the above are formed by camming the appropriate bones against the inside—and sometimes the edges—of the crack. Knee bars and thigh bars are conceptually similar to the arm-bar technique previously described.

A lesser-known technique that may be especially handy for some leaning wide cracks or flakes is a foot-and-calf combo. (Flakes are thin exfoliates of rock that are separated but still attached to the wall, forming holds or crevices that can be climbed or used for gear placement.) This entails sticking your foot inside the crack and rotating your knee inward, as if knock-kneed. That will position your calf against the opposite side of the crack from your foot or toes. Flex or straighten your ankle to fit the crack with the foot pushing one way, the calf pushing the other. Your other foot will usually smear and push against the wall while your hands are in the layback position to oppose that foot's pressure. Try this on the fifth pitch of Yosemite's *Astroman*.

Advanced Off-Width Techniques

Advanced off-width techniques require abs of steel!

Double Hands

This less commonly used technique employs both hands as one unit. The hands are placed at the same level inside the crack, back-to-back, thumbs-down. The thumb sides of the hands will cam against each other while the pinkie sides push against the sides of the crack.

Another way to do a double hand jam is to place both hands so that the palms of each face the same direction, positioning one hand with the palm covering the back of the other. The back of one hand makes contact with one side of the crack while the palm of the other hand makes contact with the crack's opposite side.

Double hand jams use both hands as one unit.

In butterfly jams, the wrists are crossed so that the backs of the hands push against each other, with thumbs up and palms to the walls.

A hand–fist combo is sometimes used when a fist alone is not wide enough to fill the crack.

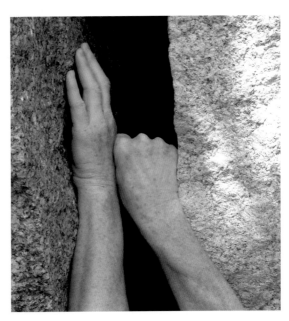

The hand can be turned toward or away from the fist in a hand–fist jam.

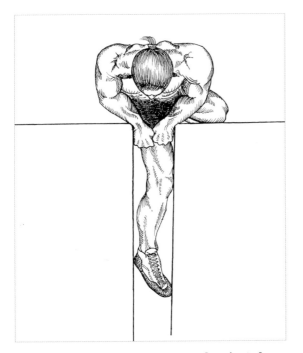

Double fist jams are most commonly oriented with palms facing down or inward.

In addition to double fists, the leg works high and deep inside the crack.

Sometimes a climber will jam one foot above the head and use a technique called Leavittation, developed by Randy Leavitt.

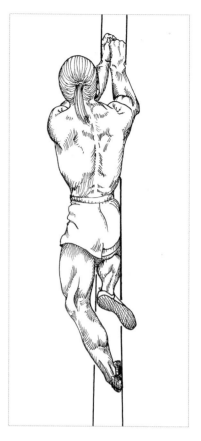

Off-width-style jams such as hand–fists or double hands work well in conjunction with a knee jam while the other foot pushes on the edge of the crack.

Butterfly

The butterfly variation is similar to the double hand technique. It turns two hands into one functioning unit. The difference is that to make a butterfly, cross your wrists and push the backs of your hands together, thumbs-up, palms to the wall.

Hand–Fist

A hand-and-fist combo is used when a fist alone is not wide enough to fill a crack. Body position, the shape or depth of the crack itself, or a wide section on a route may be too short to warrant full-fledged off-width techniques.

For a quick fix, try making a downward-facing fist and butt this against your other hand, which you can place either thumbs-up or thumbs-down in an open or cupped position. Thumbs-up is the most common version of this jam. Remember to switch hands and orientations when possible on long, continuous sections of crack. Switching will help you avoid fatigue from doing exactly the same move repeatedly.

Double Fist

Different name, same game! On routes with spots wider than double hands or hand–fist placements, have a go with double fists.

Double fists are more commonly used in the palms-inward/downward configuration, but can also work inverted. When placed side by side, palms-down, the fore knuckles and thumbs can jigsaw in a slightly offset position to form a stable, skeletal wedge.

Head Jams

These are not recommended but have been used by many desperate climbers, including at least one of the authors.

Leavittation

In the mid-1980s Tony Yaniro and Randy Leavitt developed a gravity-defying off-width technique they named Leavittation. To go to the source of inspiration, try the route *Leavittation 29* in Red Rocks, Nevada. Don't forget to pack washboard abs and aerobic fitness.

First, stack your hands in the butterfly position, as previously described, or place them overlapped, palm-to-back, with the palm of one hand pressing on one side of the crack and the back of the other hand pressing against the other. If the crack is too wide for either of these jams, make hand–fists, double fists, or the like.

Next, place one foot waist high or higher inside the crack and set a heel–toe deep inside the crack. As an alternative, jam the knee inside the crack and pull your heel toward your buttocks. (Yes, *buttocks* is as fun to type as it is to say!) Raising your heel will expand the muscles around your knee and allow you to press the joint

In a squeeze chimney, knees and palms splay out and push against the front wall while the heels, back, and buttocks work the back wall.

against the sides of the crack. Sometimes the top side of your toes or foot can scum and exert pressure against the outer wall or edge of the crack to help propel your body upward.

Your other foot pushes off the edge of the crack, face holds, or smears below while your abs

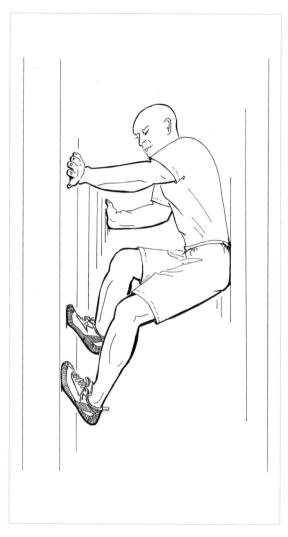

Scissoring the legs with one foot on the front wall and one behind creates opposing pressure in generous-size chimneys.

Sometimes both feet and hands are placed on the front wall while the back and buttocks oppose the pressure by pressing on the back wall.

work to keep your torso up and in toward the rock. Once securely stabilized by your abs, legs, and feet, your hands are free to be readjusted. Reset them higher, and slide your foot inside the crack up to waist level again to reset the foot jam. Repeat many times, like an inchworm. The inching process frequently continues long after you feel like puking. Some cracks are best Leavittated if you place the foot inside the crack higher than your hands—sometimes even higher than your head. To accomplish the initial foot/leg placement, it helps to rotate your torso somewhat horizontal at the same time as you lift the leg over your head.

Chimneys

Climbing a chimney can be fun or skin smoking—or both. Shirts and knee coverage are advised. The entire body can fit into these rock structures. There are two main types of chimneys. The tight-fitting kind is known as a squeeze chimney. The wider variety is simply called a chimney.

The old axiom *Inch by inch, life's a cinch* may encapsulate the correct mind-set for success in a squeeze chimney.

Tight Squeeze

The squirming moves enacted in a supertight chimney are often reminiscent of off-width techniques. Heel–toe jams, the back, and chicken-wing-style arm positions (as previously outlined) act as pressure and leverage points from which to generate upward mobility. Since double wings may be awkward or unwieldy, you may want to have one arm in a chicken wing and the other down to your side. The palm of your lower hand and your toes will rest against the front wall. Your back and heels contact the rear wall. A downward push on your hand and baby steps with the heel–toes will inch your body higher inside the chimney.

Squeeze

In a slightly wider squeeze chimney where heel–toe jams won't stick, let your legs splay out; this allows your knees to work the front wall in a coordinated effort with downward thrust on the palms of your hands. Meanwhile, your feet, buttocks, and back are pressing against the rear wall.

To slither upward, walk a foot up and press on it while thrusting down on both palms. As the push commences, unweight your back and seat momentarily. Once you've gained a measure of height, lean back against the rear wall, reset your hands, and repeat the process with the other foot.

Bigger Chimneys

More generously proportioned chimneys are easier to climb than squeeze chimneys. Following are a couple of suggested options.

For widths approximating 3 feet, the scissor method of ascension is popular. This calls for placing one leg ahead with its foot on the front wall and either hand pressed out in front. Your other leg is bent back, placing that foot on the back wall. Your other hand and hind end accompany the rear foot on the back wall. Scrunching your legs high, unweighting your behind, and then shoving off, using your feet and palms for contact, will boost your body to a new high point. Then it's time to crunch again and repeat the process. Unless the shape of the chimney dictates otherwise, it may not matter which foot, which hand, or what combination is fore and which is in the posterior position. This could be a matter of comfort and convenience. Switching positions could serve to divvy up your lactic acid load.

Sometimes you may feel inclined to place both feet ahead on the front wall while your back and derriere rest against the rear wall. The arms are then usually positioned with one to the front, one to the back, palms pushing. Alternatively, you can place both hands against the rear wall of the chimney. To drive yourself upward, engage in a motion that could be likened to a vertical waddle. One foot up, then a butt scoot, reset your hands, up with the other foot, then a butt scoot . . . and so on.

Why enjoy just one of these chimney techniques? Applying them in combination can enhance the fun.

3

Stemming, Liebacks, and Special Cracks

Stemming

Some chimneys are too wide to span with only a leg length. The natural solution is called stemming. A stem can be used in a chimney, a box, or a corner. It's also used in sport climbing, on faces, and while bouldering.

Wide Stem in a Chimney

Many people first experimented with a wide stem at about six years old, when they learned to walk their way up the inside of a door frame. By forming an X with your appendages and pressing outward against the structure, you can hold a suspended position. To ascend, you generally reposition each appendage in upward succession, while keeping steady pressure on the other three points of contact.

Wide chimneys are likely candidates for this stem. With your right hand and right foot on one wall and left hand and foot on the other, turn your palms and feet outward and alternately walk one at a time up the channel.

Picture *The Eiger Sanction*'s Clint Eastwood during his desert crack climbing session!

Stemming in a Corner

When stemming is done in a dihedral (corner), a crack for jamming fingers or hands may be involved. Whether a jam crack is available or not,

To experience stemming in a box, try El Matador (5.10d) on Devils Tower. BRIAN BAILEY

Hands or fingers may jam in the corner while the legs stem out to the sides. On a lower angle climb like this, keep your weight out over your feet by positioning your midsection away from the wall.

By forming an X with the appendages and pressing outward against the structure, this climber is able to hold a suspended position.

PART I: CRACK CLIMBING TECHNIQUES

the lower half of your body conveys itself just as in a wide stem.

Jamming creates a hybrid version of the stem. If a crack is available in the dihedral, consider varying your climbing form, from jamming your hands and feet in the crack, to a lieback (we'll discuss this a little later), to stemming your legs while jamming your hands. This effort would help you stave off a pump.

If no crack is involved other than the angle of the route's walls, the stemming fundamentals will be identical to those you learned in the door jam all those years ago: left hand and left foot on the left wall, right hand and right foot on the right wall of the dihedral.

Stemming in a Box

A box is a U-shaped formation, ordinarily with two dihedrals in the back of the recess. Boxes are standard fare at Devils Tower, Wyoming.

Stemming in a box can be just like stemming in a chimney. However, if the dihedrals provide a crack or cracks, then a hybrid technique between hand or finger jamming and stemming could be the selected course of action.

Body Bridge

If a box or chimney is too wide to span with your legs and arms in an X, like wide-open tongs, take a crack at a procedure known as body bridging.

Getting into the body-bridge position can demand gymnastic entry and exit moves. Body bridges require ample core strength in order to hold body tension.

Your goal is to have both feet on one side of the box and both hands on the other. Normally, you're facedown, with hands and head higher than your feet. To ascend, take

This climber is stemming in a Zion dihedral. On steeper climbs like this, keep your midsection closer to the wall to preserve energy. KLAUS FENGLER/RED CHILI

turns moving your hands and feet. The model sequence for progression is *hand, hand,* then *foot, foot.*

1. Body bridging involves placing both hands on one wall and both feet on the other.

2. Push with the hands and slowly move the feet higher.

3. When the feet are just below hand height, it's time to set the feet in a solid position and move the hands up again.

Liebacks

The lieback is a crucial technique to learn. Its principles come into play in every major category of climbing, including bouldering, sport climbing, steep face climbing, and, for this book, crack climbing.

Corners, offset splitters, and flakes form some of the most common routes to ascend via lieback.

The lieback creates opposing pressure between the fingers and feet. Your fingers wrap around the inside of the crack or flake and pull toward your body. The hands are customarily oriented with thumbs pointing toward each other, top hand thumbs-down, lower hand thumbs-up. Place your feet high and press away on the wall in front. The body is pushed backward by the feet and held in suspension. Imagine yourself hanging on to the side of a swimming pool, ready for a powerful push-off for the backstroke.

To move, unweight and replace one paw at a

Liebacking is a crucial technique to learn for climbing cracks.
A lieback creates opposing pressure with fingers pulling and feet pushing.

1. When liebacking, the hands can be shuffled up the crack without crossing over each other . . .

2. . . . but sometimes it's more efficient to cross the hands over, especially if the grip is secure.

time. One way to go is to keep your high hand on top and shuffle (as described in "Hand Jam") so that your arms never cross. Another choice is to move each hand successively above the other. Frequently, a combination of the two methods is used. Your feet will walk up the wall one at a time. The stride differs for various routes and climbers, depending on balance, speed, security of hand and foot placement, confidence, and so forth. The gait can be *hand, foot, hand, foot,* or *hand, hand, foot, foot.*

Undercling Cracks

An undercling is performed on a crack, edge, pocket, smear, bump, flake—et cetera!—that's upside down. When grasping the hold from underneath in an undercling, your palms are oriented either up or toward your body. The feet or some other point of your body must provide opposing pressure. An undercling is commonly held with one hand while the other reaches out and around the lip of a roof, as is done on *Ruby's Café* in

When the edge of the crack proves hard to grab, liebacking off-hand jams is another possibility.

In an undercling, grasp the hold from underneath.

Indian Creek, Utah, and *Sphinx Crack,* South Platte, Colorado.

In undercling cracks you may use similar techniques to those for vertical cracks—just turned 90 degrees. For instance, instead of lying back to the side with your fingers oriented vertically, to undercling you lean back with your fingers horizontally aligned for traversing or for reaching backward, out, or up. For undercling finger locks, slide your fingers up and into the crack, then slot them sideways. Keeping your arms flexed while holding underclings can tax your biceps. Try leaning out backward occasionally to straighten your arms, giving those big biceps a break.

Stemming, Liebacks, and Special Cracks

Fingers jam up into a slot in the rock, with palms up to hold an undercling.

Roof Cracks

A horizontal crack through an overhanging rock is called a roof crack. Roof cracks call for the same tricks as vertical cracks, but they're more strenuous.

On roof cracks, your arms and upper body hold a higher percentage of your weight than on their vertical counterparts. Your abdominal muscles must work very hard to keep your lower body elevated, so you can jam your feet in the crack. Jams must

be set securely, which may increase the time you spend placing them. The more weight they're asked to hold, the harder jams must be squeezed and bones must be cammed. The more time and exertion you spend holding on, the sooner exhaustion will hit. A major mistake is keeping your body fully extended—this is a very strenuous position. A worse error is to attempt to reach a couple of inches farther from this extended position. Being overextended can make it extremely difficult and strenuous to move a foot without swinging off. Once you've moved to a fully extended body and arms position, it's best to move your feet closer to your waist with your knees bent to remove some of the strain from your abs and back muscles.

To get a taste of roof cracks, try *Grit Roof* or *More Funky than Monkey* in Joshua Tree, California, and pack some cheese to go with the whine.

Hands and feet work the crack in Utah's Crack House.

Haute couture by Paul Piana was required for Steve Petro and Todd Skinner's FFA of Queen of the Valley, a 5.12d roof crack in Colorado, circa 1985.

Training and Resting

Cracks tend to be difficult in part because climbing them calls for such a sustained effort. One of the main reasons people fall or hang on cracks is the massive pump that often accumulates in forearms and hands. There are two ways to increase your chances for a pump-free ascent. One is to train by climbing and by lifting weights to become stronger. The other involves finding ways to rest and recover before you reach a helpless level of pump.

Training for Crack Climbing

To train forearm and hand muscles for crack climbing, nothing really beats climbing cracks—lots of them! Repeatedly holding on long enough to place gear, clip the rope, and then continue up the route requires massive endurance. For crack climbing you need both overall body strength and cardiovascular fitness. This book is not designed as a workout manual—that would be another entire book or three's worth of material—but we will present a couple of quick and easy ways to train for crack climbing.

When it's not possible to make it to the crags or the rock gym for a lactic blast, forearm and hand contractions that induce a pump similar to crack climbing can be simulated by forearm curls. Performing high numbers of repetitions in each of several sets using a barbell of moderate weight effectively builds strength and endurance in forearms and hands.

Training will be required if you want to climb Luftballondach (5.12d), the Frankenjura's premier roof crack. SEBASTIAN SCHWERTNER

One way to do forearm curls is to kneel with your forearm resting on a bench and your hand palm-up and unsupported over the bench's side. Hold a moderately heavy barbell—say, thirty pounds—and let it roll, controlled, to the tips of your fingers by opening your hand. Then contract your fingers, pulling the barbell up and rotating your hand and wrist from a down and open position to up and tightly curled. Alternatively, release and contract your hand, maintaining muscular tension and smooth control on the weight. Repeat every couple of seconds until you've achieved a nice burn. Aim for around thirty reps in the first set. If you don't reach a sufficient level of burn within twenty to thirty reps, add weight. Having two or three barbells with different weights may be useful for creating a pyramid of weight and reps: thirty pounds and thirty reps for set one, forty pounds and twenty reps for set two, fifty pounds and twelve reps for set three, forty pounds and twenty reps for set four, then back to thirty-and-thirty for set five.

Another integral part of training for climbing in general, and specifically for crack climbing, is developing abdominal and core strength. Try hanging from a pull-up bar or a leg-raise chair then raising your knees about ten times to the center, ten times to the right, ten times to the left, and another ten times to the center. Repeat sets as needed. Abs? Obliques? Just work 'em silly!

And while you're at it, why not hit the triceps, the lats, and some flexibility for hip and knee turnout?

Forearm Curl

1. Forearm curls start with the weight hanging down and fingers uncurled.

2. Forearm muscles contract as the fingers and hand curl the weight up.

Abdominal exercises, such as knee raises, develop core strength.

Leg raises also give the abs a great workout.

V-sits work the abs for core strength.

1. Scissors work the obliques and abs, first to one side . . .

2. . . . and then to the other.

Sets of lat pulls are good training for climbing.

Pulled very low, the lat bar can work triceps, too.

Resting While Crack Climbing

To make the most of strength and endurance, you must learn to be efficient and avoid becoming irrecoverably fatigued. Part of what is meant by *efficiency* is climbing quickly and confidently without error. Efficiency of this sort is learned through experience; you'll develop a repertoire of moves that you're able to perform in the proper sequence, as if intuitively.

Another part of efficiency is knowing how and when to rest. It's important to find ways and places to rest and recover whenever possible. A good rest

Finding creative ways to rest is important in all types of climbing. Here, Brian Kim takes weight off his arms by heel hooking while anticipating the next move. KLAUS FENGLER/RED CHILI

provides a reprieve from the sustained muscular contraction created by jamming, squeezing, and pulling by allowing you to stand or to hang from your skeletal system. When you relax a muscle, blood can circulate more easily to it than when it's tightly contracted. Circulation replenishes the oxygen supply and helps fend off lactic attacks. A good rest also affords the opportunity to draw your heart

and breath rates back to the comfort zone.

When you're seeking a rest, look for features in the crack like wide spots or constrictions for hands, fingers, toes, et cetera. These will be spots that are sized appropriately to lock on to the involved appendage's bones with relatively minimal muscular contraction.

For example, find a V-slot that's wide enough

to sink your hand all the way to the wrist, and also necks down so your wrist can't slide through the bottom of the V. Straighten your arm, relax the hand, and sink down into a relaxed stance to rest, breathe, and recover. If possible, let go with one hand, drop it to your side, and shake it out a little. Then switch hands and let the other one rest, shake out, and recover.

A fun way to rest in a dihedral is to straddle the corner with your feet pulled high, just below the buttocks, spread about shoulder width apart, then turn your knees inward and push them together. This forms a double knee-bar platform on which you can rest by nearly sitting on your heels. While in this position, your hands can be unweighted, partially or completely, to shake out or to place gear.

The quest for recovery may require thinking and maneuvering outside the box, literally. Jam-ming on certain cracks may become mechanical and narrow your focus to just the crack. To pursue a rest that uses different muscles or a different part of the skeleton, it may be wise to look on the face for foot- or handholds. A stem, Gaston, body scum, knee bar, or full stance may be available to those with an eye for such gems. There are incalculable numbers of ways to rest. There are as many variations as there are possible combinations of holds and body parts. Basically, stick to the rock any sensibly available part of your body that will take the strain off the part verging on fatigue.

Rests spots frequently have a point of diminishing returns. This means that at some point during the rest, you will have gleaned all the recovery that's feasible from a stance or jam and will start to expend more energy to stay in the rest spot than you're gaining in recovery. Time to go!

Resting in a Dihedral

1. An effective way to rest in a dihedral is to straddle the corner with feet pulled high just below the buttocks, spread about shoulder width apart. Turn the knees inward and push them together, forming a double knee bar.

2. Here's a top view. The double knee bar triangulates with the feet, forming a skeletal platform on which the climber can rest by almost sitting on the heels.

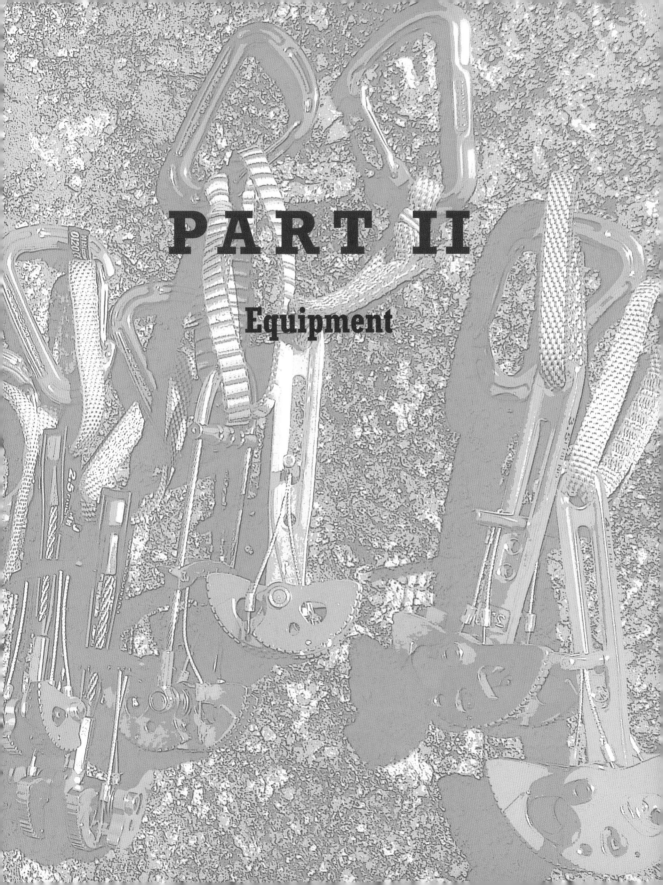

PART II

Equipment

Cams

The History of Cams

Many technological developments have changed the course and history of climbing. Just look at nylon kernmantle ropes, climbing shoes with sticky rubber on the soles—and camming devices.

Cam innovation began in 1971 by Colorado native and aerospace engineer Ray Jardine. One of the most striking examples of equipment that has enabled climbers to further their realities is the Friend—the name Jardine aptly bestowed upon his cam creations.

Here's how it happened. In 1971 Ray Jardine created a dual sliding wedge design for his own climbing use, but found it to be unsound from a safety standpoint. He then began work on a new type of device that employed constant spiral cams as the active members of the protection unit. He tested his would-be invention at his local crags, scrapping many prototypes in the process. You can almost imagine the camming unit's genesis and assembly in a secret laboratory and then stealthy

Steve Petro places a cam on **Optimator** *by
pulling the trigger with his middle finger while
pushing on the stem with his thumb, similar to
using a syringe.* BRIAN BAILEY

testing sessions at crags free of snooping eyes and inquiring minds.

Eventually Jardine came up with a design that, satisfied his criteria. In 1974, off to the Valley he went, prototype Friends in hand. The multitalented Jardine proceeded to dispatch amazing and difficult routes in Yosemite including *Crimson Cringe, Hang-dog Flyer, Separate Reality, Owl Roof, Rostrum,* and the Valley's first 5.13, *The Phoenix.* Jardine proved not only his genius as a climber, but also that his Friends were viable tools.

Ray tried unsuccessfully to solicit interest from American companies. In 1977 a climber and visionary from England, Mark Vallance, recognized the genius of Jardine's device. He and Ray came to an agreement regarding the manufacturing of Friends. In 1978 Vallance founded Wild Country and Jardine's cams soon hit the market.

Since development of camming devices first began, many variations have been made. Cams now come in dozens of sizes and numerous styles. Camming devices may fit tiny seams as small as 0.22 inch, or they may be so large that they fit

For More Information

In this section we cover the fundamentals of placing protection in cracks, but the subject of constructing solid, equalized belay anchors from natural gear is complicated and outside the scope of this book. *Climbing Anchors* by John Long and Bob Gaines offers a complete discussion of the topic.

Cams are active crack protection devices. They come in many sizes to fit diverse crack placements.

cracks of nearly 7½ inches. Jardine's innovative device probably revolutionized crack climbing more than any other single invention.

Thanks, Ray!

How Cams Work

A *cam* is defined as an asymmetrically lobed roller. For this book's purposes the cam is an "active" (meaning, having moving parts) fall protection device. It's a three- or four-lobed, spring-loaded device that pushes against the walls of a crack to protect the climber. As the spring-loaded cam lobes rotate on an axle, known as the plane of rotation, outward force is transmitted to the walls of the crack. The harder the pull on the stem, the greater pressure the cams exert against the rock at a constant 13.75-degree cam angle.

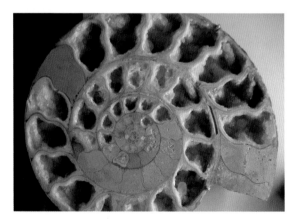

Constant cam angle is a spiral that is an expression of uniform growth. Logarithmic spirals can be found in seashells, pinecones, spiral nebulas, and climbing gear.

To envision the meaning of the term *cam angle,* picture a cam placed in a vertical, parallel-sided crack with its stem vertically aligned and contacting the smooth vertical walls. Then draw a horizontal line through the center of the axle, outward to the two sides of the crack. (Where this horizontal line intersects the walls of the crack, it will be perpendicular to the vertical walls.) Next, draw another line from the center of the axle to the point on the cam lobe where it makes contact with the wall of the crack. These two lines intersect in the axle, and the angle formed is 13.75 degrees. Various angles were tested during Jardine's prototype phase. After extensive trials and applications both at the crags and in the factory in England, 13.75 degrees was determined to be and remains the internationally accepted, definitive cam angle.

For a more in-depth look at cam angle, look no farther than Descartes' and Bernoulli's studies of the logarithmic spiral, aka *spira mirabilis* or marvelous spiral. A logarithmic spiral is a constant curve that comes from a central point, growing progressively farther away from the center as it revolves around the point of origin. As the spiral line revolves, the size of the logarithmic spiral increases, but its angle is unchanged with successive growth. The spira mirabilis can be witnessed in nature growing in sunflowers, nautilus shells, and pinecones.

How to Operate a Cam

There are three main parts on a camming device: the cams, the trigger, and the stem, which has a sling and carabiner attached to it.

To place a cam, pull on the trigger while pushing on the stem, like a gigantic syringe. The butt of the stem fits into the palm of your hand while your fingers straddle the stem and manipulate the trigger bar. Pulling on the trigger retracts the spring-loaded cams. With cams retracted, the head of the cam is

Example of a well-placed cam. Logarithmic spirals found on camming devices used in crack climbing have a constant cam angle of 13.75 degrees.

Usually the most secure fit is found on the tightest (most retracted) third of the lobe's expansion range.

then inserted into the crack at the chosen spot.

The stem should be aligned to the direction from which your impact would load the camming device if you fell. The goal is to line up the stem with the point of impact so that the cams will take the force of the fall most directly, thereby avoiding torsion on the stem.

When your fingers leave the trigger, the cams snap open to fill the width of the crack. You then clip the rope through the carabiner attached to the stem's sling.

To remove a cam, work the procedure in reverse by first grasping and retracting the cams via pulling on the trigger. The unit will slide out of the placement, reversing the path it used to enter. Clip it back on your rack, ready for the next go.

Where Cams Work

Cams can be placed in vertical, horizontal, diagonal, or roof cracks. They fit well into parallel-sided cracks where passive chocks would not stick. Cams work well placed straight up, overhead, even in a parallel-sided roof crack. Nothing can rival a camming device in this situation! Cams can also be fitted into pods, constrictions, or even flaring spots if you take proper care that the cams all contact the crack's surface within a safe range on the lobe's rand. Again, all the cam lobes should have good contact with the sides of the crack.

The best fit is the most secure fit. Usually, the most secure fit is found on approximately the tightest, most retracted third of the lobe's expansion range. However, cams should not be placed in the maximum-tight position. If you retracted such a cam completely and then place it in the constriction with contact on the very tightest, inner part of the lobe, the device could be stuck there permanently or may require great effort to remove. This happens because to remove the spring-loaded cam, you must pull the trigger mechanism. The lobes must be released from their expanded fit inside the crack. If the cams are already fully retracted, there's no pull left in the system.

The middle third of the lobe range is acceptable if there's no danger of the cam "walking" or being kicked from its original placement and the cam has been placed in solid, stationary rock.

It's best to think of the outer, most open third of the range as a backup for the middle third, but *not* as the desired part of the cam on which to stake the placement. The backup will provide play for cams that walk out of the intended placement or get kicked or pulled by rope friction.

Walking means the cams are placed loosely enough that vibration or jostling can wiggle each pair independently deeper into the crack. Sometimes cams are placed too loosely by an inexperienced or unobservant leader. Other times they're placed in a crack that's too flaring. In either instance they are suspect and may walk to a wider spot where the lobes no longer fit the crack tightly enough to hold a climber's weight. If they walk to a spot too wide to hold them at all, the unit may simply tumble out of the crack altogether.

Whether or not you're a frequent flier on lead, it's sensible to seek a secure placement. Place cams tight, as a general rule, but not so tight that they become permanent features of the crack.

If you place cams horizontally or diagonally, take care that any rigid portion of the stem is not situated over the edge of the crack such that it could be subject to snapping due to leverage under severe load.

See chapter 7 for further discussion about placing cams.

Safety

Always read and understand the instructions that are supplied with lifesaving climbing equipment. Always check safety equipment before each use. If you're in doubt about the condition of any piece of gear on your rack, or any safety equipment at all, retire it from further use immediately and permanently. This does not mean sell it or give it to an unsuspecting climber looking for a deal.

Retirement indicators to look for on cams and nuts include, but are not limited to, corrosion, burrs, cracks, distortion, broken or frayed or distorted wires and cables, or any other form of excessive wear or abrasion. Terminal textile damage to slings and harnesses might include such symptoms as melted, abraded, sun-damaged, chemically damaged, broken, or worn threads or fibers.

Cams deteriorate over time as a normal aging process. The life span of climbing equipment is subject to its use and environmental factors, as well as actual age.

Addressing the issue of retirement and obsolescence for camming devices, one climbing hardware manufacturer noted:

Official response must be in line with European regulations for PPE (Personal Protective Equipment). All of this company's climbing equipment is now type tested and certified to an EN standard, part of which covers obsolescence. The specific information from our current instruction manual is quoted below:

Obsolescence: This product will deteriorate over time in the course of normal use and because of this we are required by directive 89/686/EEC to give an obsolescence date. It is difficult to be precise but a conservative estimate for this product is that it has a life span of 10 years from date of first use for metal components, or 5 years from date of first use or 10 years from date of first storage for textile components. However, please note that the following factors will further reduce the safe working life of the product.

Metal components: Normal use, exposure to chemical reagents, heat contamination, high impact load or failure to maintain (clean/lubricate) as recommended.

Textile components: Most textile components are known to degrade gradually with time even when stored in ideal conditions. Additionally normal use, rope burn, exposure to elevated temperatures, high impact load, prolonged exposure to UV light including sunlight, abrasion, cuts or failure to maintain (clean) as recommended will cause further reduction in strength.

What all the above means is that cams manufactured more than 10 years ago will not be repaired in any way and we advise that for your safety, any equipment covered by the above should be withdrawn from use. Cams manufactured more than 10 years ago should be withdrawn from further use, your life may depend on it.

Use your head; do the math! A shopping trip at your local climbing store will be a lot cheaper and more fun than even a quick trip to the emergency room!

Maintenance of Cams

Cam maintenance entails inspection, cleaning and lubricating where relevant, and proper storage.

To inspect cams, do a safety check as outlined in the previous section of this book. You should also do an operational check, which includes ensuring that the unit operates smoothly throughout its complete expansion range. Check, too, that when the trigger is released from any point, all cam lobes snap back to the fully open position.

To rid cams of the grime and grit that inhibit smooth action, rinse them in warm water of drinking quality. If the grit doesn't rinse out, wash the head of the cam in warm soapy water, retracting and releasing the trigger to help loosen dirt. The water temperature should not exceed 104 degrees F. Be sure to keep the sling dry and away from any soap or detergent. Thoroughly rinse all soap from the device and towel-dry it immediately. Then allow it to completely dry in a warm room, away from direct heat.

Lubrication—WD-40 or something similar—should be applied to the springs and to the juncture of the axle and cams. Retract and release the trigger bar until a smooth cam action is attained. Wipe all excess lubricant from the device. Absolutely do not allow any lubricant or any chemical residue of any kind to contact the sling material or rope.

If a chemical solution, powder, or residue of any kind comes into contact with the sling material, send the unit to a credible sling-sewing repair facility before using it further.

Gear should be stored unpacked and tangle-free. It should be kept in dry, dark, cool, ventilated conditions. Keep it away from sharp edges, corrosives, pressure, and all other potentially damaging elements.

CHAPTER SIX

Nuts and Hexes

Overview of Nuts and Hexes

From the time when Rogers and Ripley pounded wooden stakes into crevices on Devils Tower, Wyoming, for a first ascent on the Fourth of July, 1893, climbers have sought to develop hardware that would make the sport safer.

In the early 1900s German and Italian climbers developed pitons and carabiners for the fledgling sport. Throughout much of Europe and the United States, rock-scarring pitons became the staple protection device. Pitons are thick, blade-shaped metal units pounded into a crack. They have an eyelet on the outer end through which to clip a carabiner or thread webbing. Pitons are systematically hammered into a rock crevice, and hammered out again after use on the pitch. This is a very strenuous procedure from a free stance—and it's also quite damaging to the rock.

Climbers tied shoelaces and ropes around rocks that were lodged inside cracks to use as protection points. Others tied knots, forming loops of cord. These knots were fitted onto cracks, and the loop end was clipped with a carabiner. Knots were used as fall protection in the same way that metal nuts are used. In Elbsandstein, Germany, climbers still use cord knots, because metal gear is forbidden.

In 1927 Fred Pigott experimented with cords threaded through machine nuts for protection on crack routes on the Black Cliff of the Black Height, Clogwyn Du'r Arddu, on Snowdon near Llanberis, Wales. After World War II British climbers used these threaded machine nuts and dispensed with piton hammering. In the early 1970s Yvon Chouinard, after numerous climbing trips to

A Brief History

In the beginning man had no rock climbing hardware, no nuts to bear, no hexes at all. Seeing that he was unprotected, man invented specialized tools for his new pastime, rock climbing. Then other men went on to mass-produce specially formed nuts swaged on steel wire; and climbers saw that nuts were good.

Britain, returned to the United States and began manufacturing aluminum wedges to use as crack protection in lieu of steel pitons. Eventually these morphed into what we now call nuts, usually swaged on steel wire rather than threaded cord as in the old days.

What Are Nuts and Hexes?

Nuts and hexes are "passive" (meaning they have no moving parts) gear for fall protection. *Nut* is a generic term for a chock that wedges into a constriction in rock to protect a climber. Nuts have four sides and a top and a bottom. A hex is a six-sided nut with two ends that's used similarly to a standard nut. Both hexes and nuts are pierced with holes through which cord or cable is then fastened. Sometimes the cable forms a complete loop and is fastened by swaging. In other constructions a cable may be soldered into the base of the nut. A carabiner is clipped through the end loop on the cord or cable and the rope is clipped through the biner while the nut is in use on a route.

Nuts often come in multiple colors these days to allow quick identification of different sizes.

Nuts are usually slung with high-tensile-strength stainless-steel cables. These cables are very strong. The steel cable is very durable, too, so long as it is not bent severely, crimped, abraded, or frayed. Repetitive motion from bending over a severe angle on the same point on a cable can damage it, although the damage may be invisible to the naked eye. It's wise to recognize and keep track of forces that have been applied to individual pieces of

Racking up with a good selection of nuts and cams to climb cracks in the mist on Clogwyn Du'r Arddu, Wales.

gear on your rack. To be prudent, perform a routine, commonsense safety evaluation of each piece on your rack and all other climbing safety equipment.

Nuts have widely replaced the use of pitons. Pitons are steel spikes that are hammered into a rock crevice for protection. They're still used on some aid climbs, but their use on free climbs has been adamantly shunned for more than three decades. Widespread use of pitons was like a juggernaut that over time seriously displaced so much rock, it has completely changed the character of many routes that have existed since the 1950s.

Nuts are far less damaging to the rock, and for free climbing and many aid applications, they are

Hexes are six-sided nuts with two ends that wedge into a constriction in a crack.

more efficient than their piton predecessors. They're also less strenuous to place and remove than hammering a piton. Placing nuts instead of pitons eliminates the need to carry a three-pound hammer dangling from your waist. Free-climbing grades were significantly raised as a result of nut-protected climbs.

For the larger, more complexly shaped hexes, it's most appropriate to use a high-tensile-strength cord instead of wire cable to thread the unit. In the case of the hex, a flexible cord or sling material allows maximum seating potential on all sides. Hexes can be placed on any side, as needed to fit the constriction. Depending on the shape of the crack and the orientation of the hex within the placement, fiber slings typically conform better to bends and turns that are forced on them than wire cables do. If placed in a way that the wire cable is

flexed, the somewhat resilient nature of the wire strand may seem to poke the unit out of its intended placement. If the hex stays put but you fall on a bent wire, the cable may become damaged permanently if it gets crimped or frayed. Another advantage to hexes on slings is that slings can be replaced more easily than wire should the need arise.

Hexes take a bit longer to place than Friends, so a leader may look to place them in relatively easier sections of the climb and save the Friends for the more difficult sections. So why—you may be asking—do climbers use hexes at all if Friends can be placed faster? Well, hexes are about one-third the cost of camming units, as well as being lighter compared with similar-size cams. One true advantage of a hex over a camming unit is its resistance to rotating and walking as the leader climbs past.

Most folks who have climbed cracks have heard stories or seen instances in which cams have walked so deeply into a crack, they've become useless or irretrievably stuck. Hexes do not walk back into a crack. Well-placed hexes stay put; poorly placed hexes are dislodged and fall out of the crack, sliding down the rope to come to rest dangling atop the next protection piece.

Hexes slung on webbing fiber, such as Dyneema, are better than wired hexes because they are more readily placed in passive camming configurations on any paired facets of the unit. Wired hexes, especially in the smaller sizes, can hinder secure placement or can sometimes get in the way, preventing placement altogether.

The advantage of a wired hex (as compared with a hex slung with webbing) is that the stiff wire allows it to be placed a few inches higher. In some cases those few inches may mean the difference between a placement from an easy stance and a higher jam from a more strenuous position.

Where Nuts and Hexes Work

This section is all about the rock and crack shapes that accept nuts and hexes. More specifics regarding placing gear in a variety of special rock features will be discussed in chapter 7.

Cracks are found in every kind of rock that's good to climb. Most climbers think of granite cracks—and for good reason, since hundreds of thousands of climbers visit California's Yosemite Valley and Joshua Tree National Park every year. Granite is host to some of the world's most famous climbing areas and most renowned cracks. It's standard to travel to these areas bearing full sets of nuts, offset nuts, hexes, and cams.

Others may think primarily of soft sandstone cracks in Utah. Sandstone aficionados, who climb

Nuts and hexes work best when placed in a constriction rather than a parallel-sided or flaring crack. This hex is slotted just right.

A V-slot offers an ideal nut placement.

parallel-sided cracks, commonly use camming units to the exclusion of nuts or hexes.

Limestone cracks are typically bolted, since many are located in sport-climbing areas. If they're not bolted, then nuts, hexes, and cams may be appropriate fare, depending on the individual crack.

Basalt cracks can be found many places, including Arizona, Oregon, and Idaho. These cracks tend to be quite parallel and are usually well protected by cams rather than nuts or hexes.

Nuts and hexes work best when placed into crack constrictions, as opposed to parallel-sided or flaring cracks. The ideal nut placement spot is a V-slot. A nut in a V-slot will tend to become wedged even more securely than when initially placed if it becomes weighted as in an aid situation, or when it takes the brunt of a lead fall. In contrast, a nut placed in a constriction that is too slight may deform and pull out when fallen on, or may simply chatter out of placement and become useless.

Very few cracks provide perfect V-slots repeatedly for the entire pitch. One exception is the *Walt Bailey Memorial Route* at Devils Tower—a beautiful example of perfect V-slots through the whole pitch. Nope, Devils Tower is not granite or basalt. Flip back to the "Rocks and Cracks" section in the beginning of the book if you don't remember.

Frequently, cracks provide constrictions that aren't perfect, but are sufficient for safe nut placement. Lead climbing on the bulletproof Fountain Sandstone cliffs at Eldorado Canyon near Boulder, Colorado, provides an excellent opportunity for practicing nut placement in deceptive, unobvious rock constrictions. Curved nuts and offset nuts work very well in an area like this; don't go without them.

Not all granite is created equal. In some areas, such as Vedauwoo, the granite is composed of large crystals that make for a very bumpy and rough-feeling stone. This granite grates the skin more than its Fremont Canyon or Yosemite counterparts. The large crystals often provide an excellent opportunity for finding creative constrictions. *Creative* here means that you need to observe the subtle bumps within the general rock shape to find the best constriction for nut placement. Rather than two sides of

the crack moving toward each other to create a V-slot, these large crystals are often found at similar levels on opposite sides of the crack. The crystals choke the crack, providing a spot for nut placement. It's usually better to set curved nuts so that the concave side is against the larger of two crystals.

Nuts tend to work better than cams in shallow cracks. If only two cams of a three-cam unit (or only three cams of a four-cam unit) fit into the crack, this is a clear indicator that trying to place a nut or hex may be the better choice. Even if a cam could fit deeply enough, sometimes the shape of the rock prohibits the cam stem from being rotated downward to its correct position. This is another indicator that a nut or hex may fit better. Furthermore, the rock doesn't always devour a nut to the climber's satisfaction. Most of the time you must fiddle with the placement, wiggling the nut this way and that so it fits past the intricate features of the crack into the sweet spot. If a guidebook warns that nut placement is tricky or difficult, the above examples are the kinds of issues you must be prepared for.

If you're going to attempt a wily route with tricky placements, it's best to first test yourself on a route rated a full number grade below your comfort zone. The main reason for this is that each placement will take more time to work through—specifically, more time to see or find the spot, choose the correct-size nut, and then fiddle the nut into the complicated features of the rock. A route that throws five to ten of these crafty nut placements at you taxes your physical and mental strength, for sure. It's possible that toproping such a route may feel easy compared with leading the same climb. Placing pro on lead is integral to the difficulty and grade of crack climbs.

One unique crack shape is a slightly flaring shallow crack; here, a camming unit will not fit completely and securely. This shape can be natural or human-made by the use of steel pitons, hammered into and then out of the same spot for hundreds or thousands of ascents—removing enough material not only to increase the size of the crack but also to alter its shape. In most cases offset nuts (aluminum or brass) fit very well in pin scars or slightly flared cracks. Especially for climbers who are new to using offsets and who have minimal experience at protecting pin scars and flares, it takes more time to select the proper-size offset nut and find the most secure placement than it does to place a simple wedge or curved nut in a V-slot.

When attempting a route like *Serenity Crack* in Yosemite, be prepared for a unique challenge in protecting the flared pin scars. Another route only slightly scarred from pins, but still requiring more time spent wiggling small wired nuts, is *Green Adjective* in Utah's Little Cottonwood Canyon. Please take offset nuts before attempting to lead these two

Many routes in Fremont Canyon are situated directly over the river, like **Morning Sickness (5.11d)**.

The Case for Extension Slings

One day I was near the top of Fremont Canyon's *Wine and Roses,* where I placed a size 1 Friend because I didn't have a size 1.5 (which would have been the best fit). Stupidity should be painful, and so the gods see to it that it is. I fell off and ripped the size 1 Friend from the rock. The two cams below were deep in the crack and *should've* had extenders, but didn't; as a result, they rotated completely out of the crack. Yup, I took a 50-foot screamer because the vector (direction part) on the two cams below the top cam rotated them into compromised positions (with the stem facing straight out rather than down toward the center of the earth). The vector (magnitude part) pulled the compromised cams out with the force from my weight and the distance fallen. Luckily, pride was all that was hurt: My fall ended 100 feet above the deck.

Learning to match shapes in the crack with the appropriate type, shape, size, and orientation of gear is a serious skill to develop. Make the time!

—Steve Petro

routes. The search-and-rescue teams will appreciate it. In the olden days they were led without offsets because offsets had yet to be invented. Climbers today have the safety advantage of a more diverse range of gear to protect specific shapes of cracks. You can choose to ignore our suggestion that you carry offset nuts on pin-scarred routes, of course—just like you can disregard the warning label on a pack of cigarettes.

Some crack shapes are not conducive to nut placement. Avoid placements in outward-flaring cracks, where the nut will simply pop out. This is especially true if the crack is at all overhanging.

Avoid placements in cracks that flare inward to the degree that gear may fall backward into the crack and become useless in any number of different ways, not to mention irretrievable. However, there are times when a nut placed inside an inward-flaring crack, then pulled forward toward the surface and set with a firm tug, can be seated very securely near the edge of the crack.

Avoid placements in downward-flaring cracks where the nut is lucky just to stay put even without the added challenge of holding a fall.

V-slots that are too obtuse may make contact with the bottom of the nut but not significant and secure contact with its sides. If it's resting on its bottom, the nut is unstable and could easily fall out of the placement. Avoid V-slots that are too obtuse to properly pinch the sides of a nut.

Avoid bottoming out placements where the nut wedges nicely but the constriction is too thin to accept the wire cable. It is highly preferable that the cable point down toward the ground, rather than toward your chest. A nut placed with the cable bent and poking out will lift or pop out too easily, as the rope passing through the biner pulls up on the nut's cable while the leader climbs past.

When that happens—a nut pulls out of the crack as you climb past—it slides down the rope to the last placement. Most of the time this is farther down than you care to downclimb to retrieve your fallen nut. On the other hand, climbing farther without pro could be gambling with a very nasty fall.

Whether you're ascending a vertical crack, tra-versing a horizontal crack, or chugging through a roof crack, always consider the vector potential on each nut and cam you place. In physics a *vector* is defined as a force possessing magnitude and direction. This means you must be aware of the direction of gravity's pull on every nut in the pitch. Consider, too, that all the placements below the top nut might influence the vector on that top nut if you fall on it. It's not realistic to outline every possible scenario in this book, of course. Still, things like quickdraws or over-the-shoulder slings on certain placements, or the lack of these extenders, influence the vector on a nut you fall upon, and possibly other placements as well.

Placing Nuts and Hexes

Nut and hex placement is an art form. The ability to create high-quality art becomes well developed through acute attention to detail and regular practice. This art requires several steps. First, you—the leader—must look sharply at the crack, mentally logging its details (size and shape). Second, you

Nut Placement

1. Here, the leader slots a wired nut just above head level but within eye-shot for close inspection of the placement.

must select the size of nut or hex from your rack to properly fit the undulation you're targeting (first try is the goal). The third step is placing the wedge securely within the crevice. Then you set the nut, clip it, and go.

It's all too easy to become frozen with confusion, thinking about the placed pro rather than climbing onward. Such second thoughts may stem from apprehensions about the gear you've placed, rational or not. You may know that you haven't placed gear well but find yourself hesitating over how—or even whether—to make necessary adjustments. This confusion has its costs.

It takes time and consumes stamina to make pro placement revisions. If you become pumped while readjusting gear, the risk of a lead fall higher on the route increases. Some leaders in this situation choose to forsake the readjustment to conserve strength (to avoid a pump), hoping to finish the route in good style—or at least complete the next higher placement before falling or hanging. Others will opt to sort out a better gear placement, risk

becoming pumped, and then hang if necessary before continuing up the crack.

Even when your pro placement is good or bomber, you may find yourself worrying about what-ifs. The importance of placing pro well, placing it quickly, deciding to trust it, and then climbing onward with confidence cannot be stressed enough. If you doubt your gear, you're distracted from the climb ahead. Focus!

There is small disproportion betwixt a fool who useth not wit because he hath it not and him that useth it not when it should avail him.
—Queen Elizabeth I, 1587

Nuts

To place a nut, hold on to the wire and slide the device into the rock crevice. It's a good idea to set the aluminum wedge by pulling down on the wire with a firm tug to seat the nut in the rock's con-

2. The racked nuts and the carabiner are then separated from the placed nut.

3. A quickdraw is attached to the placed nut, and the rope is clipped into the bottom carabiner.

striction. As you might expect, larger wedges with greater surface area are potentially easier to place and provide a higher level of security. To place smaller wedges—say, Rock size 3 and smaller—it takes more time to find a secure constriction, and there's less wiggle room for the small piece of aluminum to fit. In most cases curved nuts offer more opportunities to fit well than straight-sided nuts. Curves on nuts' surfaces fit bumps and rounded indentations inside cracks better than straight-sided nuts. Curved sides can also help cause a camming action between the nut and the rock. This action enhances the pro's holding power within the placement by camming harder as weight from hanging or falling is applied.

There are both major- and minor-axis nut placements. Think of the major axis as holding the wider faces of the unit; these are the primary faces to make contact with the rock. The minor axis has the narrower sides of the unit that less frequently come into rock contact. The top surface of a nut is usually trapezoidal or rectangular in shape. The strength ratings may differ from major to minor axis, so as with any other gear, it's prudent to consider whether or not the strength of a unit is appropriate in a given application.

Nuts are most commonly placed on the major axis, identified by the nut's paired, curved faces; it usually fits a narrower constriction than the minor axis. This is because the faces of the major axis are the nut's wider faces, to allow maximum surface contact with the rock. If a curved nut almost fits a crack but not quite, try turning it 180 degrees. The irregularities on one side of the crack may fit the nut's concave side best, or they may call for its convex side.

Nuts can also be placed on the minor axis. This axis typically fits a

The upper nut is placed on its minor axis, and the nut below it is placed on the major axis.

slightly wider constriction than the major axis. If a constriction is just a little too wide to securely hold a nut placed in the major axis, try turning the nut 90 degrees to the minor. It may now fit into the slightly wider spot, though the trade-off could be significantly decreased surface area, depending on the nut's shape. The rock-contacting sides of the minor axis aren't as deep as the faces of the major axis are wide, so the minor axis offers less contact between nut and rock.

Hexes

Hexes are formed by three pairs of opposing, off-parallel sides of different heights. A hex is six-sided and has two ends. Viewed from the end, it looks like an asymmetrical hexagon. Like nuts, hexes are manufactured in curved or straight-sided versions. Also like curved nuts, curved hexes may fit better if

the concave side faces, for example, to the right respective to the right wall of the crack. Conversely, they might fit better with the convex side facing right, depending on the overall shape of the target spot in the crack and by any bumps and crystals on the crack's inside walls. When the hex is turned 90 degrees, the ends provide a nut-type placement.

No matter what direction you place a hex, look carefully to be sure it's seated in the intended position within the crack. Pulling firmly on the sling will set the hex and ensure that it stays as placed, in the selected orientation.

As with curved nuts, the curved sides of hexes cause a passive camming action between the unit and the rock. Here, *passive* refers to the fact that nuts and hexes have no moving parts. On devices simply referred to as cams, the camming is active, meaning that cams have moving parts. (See chapter

This hex is placed on the major axis.

Hexes can also be placed on the minor axis.

5 for more about cams.) Camming action enhances the pro's holding power within the placement by exerting increasingly stronger outward pressure against the walls of the crack as an increasing amount of weight from hanging or falling is applied.

Determining the Value of Placements

How can you tell a good placement from one that's not reliable? Let's find out. To start with, placements can be labeled in four ways: bomber, good, marginal, and bad.

A **bomber** nut makes significant surface contact with the rock constriction about a quarter to half of the way from the bottom to the top of the wedge. Nope, you don't have to take a ruler on the climb;

This bomber nut has lots of surface contact with the rock.

just learn to eyeball it. There's a lot of surface-area contact between the sides of the nut and the rock in a bomber placement. It won't pull from the crack even in the event of a high-impact fall, unless the forces applied to the nut exceeds the rated strength of the unit. Unfortunately, once the limits of the materials have been exceeded, deformation of the wedge will occur—which may allow the mangled blob to pull from the crack. Even if it does manage to stay within the crack, under rare and extreme circumstances, the cable could eventually break.

A **good** placement sits in the constriction about a quarter to two-thirds of the way from the bottom to the top of the wedge. A good placement probably won't pull from the crack even from a long fall.

In a **marginal** placement the wedge contacts the crack about two-thirds to three-quarters of the way from the nut's bottom to its top. A marginal placement stands a chance of holding a short fall—or not, especially if the nut is small. Even assuming a placement just as competent as with a larger nut, a small model is apt to fail with greater frequency thanks to its inherently fractional amount of surface contact and potential deformation of its minimal material. Placements of small nuts may also fail given even minute rock damage from weight or impact.

There are lots of ways to place **bad** gear. For example, a nut that sits about seven-eighths of the way from the bottom to the top of the wedge is prone to rotating out of the crack as you move past it, since it's not securely seated. A nut placed with its only significant contact too close to the top should be considered suspect: It could easily wiggle from the intended placement, or it could deform and pull from the crack were you to fall.

Engaging a nut's bottom surface—rather than its sides—against the constriction of rock is also bad. A nut resting on its bottom is perched on its placement rather than actively, appropriately engaged within the placement. A perched nut is likely to rotate or to be lifted out of its site as you climb above it. An exception could be a nut whose cable has been threaded through a hole or a tiny slot so that the nut cannot be removed again with-

1. When cleaning or seconding a route, first remove the gear from the crack.

2. Next, unclip it from the rope.

out unthreading the cable. Such a nut could rest on its bottom and yet be valuable protection.

A nut set against a sizable rugosite (a rough surface feature) is in a potentially marginal to bad placement. This is because the nut could rotate or teeter against the crystal point. Furthermore, if the crystal snapped off, the nut would lose its point of contact and pop from the placement.

Avoid placements where part of the wedge protrudes from the side of the crack. A protruding nut has less potential surface area with which to contact the rock.

In summary, your goal is to get as much surface contact between the sides of the nut and the rock as possible.

How to Remove Nuts and Hexes

Okay, so the leader has placed nuts and hexes to protect the ascent. But how does the second climber, who follows the pitch, remove (or clean) the gear from the rock?

3. Finally, clip the removed gear to your racking loops.

The nut tool pushes up on the nut to help remove it from the constriction. Nuts can also be removed before the rope and quickdraw are unclipped, thus minimizing the danger of dropping the nut.

If you're that second, you must find a stance where it's relatively easy to release one hand's grip from the crack, use it to remove the nut or hex, and finally place the pro on your harness gear loop or gear sling. Sometimes you'll only have time (or strength) to remove the gear before a fall feels imminent. In this case it's best to let the wedge and carabiner ride on the rope and climb to an easier section before stowing them away.

Whenever possible, alternate hands as you remove pro. Otherwise, if one hand is always gripping the rock, it may get prematurely pumped. You'll likely fall or give up and release your grip on the rock.

To remove units on wire, pinch the wire very near the bottom of the wedge and wiggle the unit out of the constriction. If it doesn't budge, grasp the carabiner and exert an upward tug. If the wedge moves, revert to your first attempt, pinching and wiggling.

If the leader has welded the piece by tugging too hard when setting it, or by falling on it, more intense measures are required. One such measure is using a nut tool—a blade-shaped lever—to strike the bottom and/or side of the nut. Some nut tools come equipped with handles that significantly increase grip comfort, although tools with handles weigh more than the Spartan kind. Because a handle provides better grip and more comfort when striking a nut, your chances of dislodging a stuck nut are increased. You can also use a nut tool to apply leverage to a unit: Pry up from the bottom to pop the gear upward and out. A good nut tool will have a hooked snout, which you can sometimes

work under the wire atop the wedge. By pulling the wire up through the wedge, you may be able to wrap a finger or a carabiner through the cable above the wedge and yank it from the top.

If the nut tool doesn't do the trick, clip the carabiner or quickdraw connected to the nut onto your harness's belay loop. Then climb up above it to apply upward pressure. If you still can't dislodge the stubborn nut and have to leave it behind, it becomes fair booty for the next climber.

Safety Inspection

We've said this before, but it bears repeating: Always read and understand the instructions that are supplied with lifesaving climbing equipment. Check your safety equipment before each use. If you're in any doubt about the condition of a piece of gear on your rack, or any safety equipment at all, retire it from further use immediately and permanently. This does not mean sell it or give it to an unsuspecting climber looking for a deal.

Retirement indicators to look for on nuts and hexes include, but are not limited to, corrosion, burrs, cracks, distortion, broken or frayed or distorted wires and cables, or any other form of excessive wear or abrasion. Textile damage to slings on nuts and hexes might include such symptoms as melted, abraded, sun-damaged, chemically damaged, broken, or worn threads or fibers.

Nuts and hexes deteriorate over time as part of the normal aging process. The life span of climbing equipment depends on its use and environmental factors as well as its actual age.

More About Placing Protection

Learning to Place Pro

A great way to practice nut and cam placement is while standing on the ground. Place the pro, with an attached sling, into the crack. Step into the sling with your full weight and watch what the nut or cam does. Sometimes nothing appears to happen and the gear seems very stable, in a solid placement. Other times the cam can be seen shifting a bit—and it may expand into a very secure spot. A nut, too, may slip deeper into the constriction, becoming even more secure than when first placed. Conversely, when movement of a placed cam or nut occurs, it may become unstable and could pull or even fall from the rock.

Practice placing gear and experimenting by applying force to it from various directions, on every shape of crack you can find. By observing the results of the experimental placements, you'll eventually learn what looks good, what looks marginal, and what looks bad. Analyzing pro while standing on the ground is a sound test method. Testing pro as the result of a lead fall gives far more conclusive proof of whether the gear placement was of the good, the bad, or the ugly variety.

Leading is very serious business. Do not attempt to lead a climb until you have received ample, hands-on instruction from an experienced guide or a credibly experienced climber. Rock climbing is no safer than driving, yet climbers have no required schools to attend, no official tests to pass, no diploma or license to receive. Drivers, of course, must pass numerous driving skills tests after having received instruction from a certified teacher who sits in the car next to the neophyte. Until pro is tested with a lead fall, climbers are only working within the safe confines of theory. Only an experienced leader knows for sure what well-placed protection is, and which protection is false. It's our opinion that only through weighting or falling on the gear can anyone truly be an experienced leader. Until then, you're only trusting in theory. Remember the adage that is so often repeated after a misfortune: *Chalk it up to experience.* Experience is gained, on occasion, through mishaps and errors.

> *They are most deceived that trusteth most in themselves.*
> —QUEEN ELIZABETH I, 1549

Deciding to Risk a Fall

Deciding to risk a lead fall is the climber's choice, and should always be decided on personally, rather than from peer pressure or other external factors.

Naturally, you don't have the same luxury of time if you're leading that you enjoy while standing on the ground. In haste, pro can be placed haphazardly. In panic mode, pro can be placed poorly. After numerous leads and years of climbing, you may still never have fallen on or weighted gear that you've placed on trad routes. In this case you'll probably think of yourself as an experienced leader,

Six Star Crack (5.13b) is a beautiful line with a skyscape to match. BRIAN BAILEY

Racked and ready, the leader commits to Bird of Fire (5.10a), Joshua Tree.

perhaps having led many routes in many different areas without falling. However, you're most likely leading routes well within your comfort zone. Assessing risk against potential glory is—again—the individual climber's choice, and should always be decided personally.

> *Good judgment comes from experience, and often experience comes from bad judgment.*
> —RITA MAE BROWN

Learning to Fall

Pushing difficulty levels in climbing is largely limited by your willingness to accept growing risk. The word *difficulty* may indicate harder grades or new types of climbing that you haven't experienced. People's tolerance for risk seems to develop at various rates. Moving to harder routes or higher grades naturally increases the chance of falling, and some climbers are very cautious when wading into deepening risk while others dive right in. Who's to say how fast is correct? However, testing and pushing personal limits is mandatory if you want to reach your full potential. Like risk, limits are mutable. They expand or contract as you gain experience and knowledge, and as your attitude changes. A true and full level of expertise is developed through continually testing your skills in various situations. In other words, it requires leaving your comfort zone or stepping out of the box. They don't call it trial *and error* for nothing!

If you've never experienced a lead fall, you've never tested your gear to see whether it's trustworthy or not. Thus it can be beneficial to take calculated falls on well-placed nuts and cams. To set up this scenario, climb 20 to 30 feet with protection placed every body length. Then, with your belayer on notice, let go of the rock and let your weight fall onto the highest piece—in this scenario, approximately at waist height.

You may prefer to make this test using gear placed by an experienced leader. Here, the leader lowers to the ground from the same 20- to 30-foot section with gear placed every body length. Then you yo-yo (leave your gear and rope in place) to the high point of the climb and—with the belayer on notice—let go. If the leader is happy, the next step is to up the ante by climbing higher above the gear, so that the nearest pro is about knee or ankle level, then let go. At some point you'll no longer need to continue this testing phase. The main point here is to create confidence by using a scientific approach. It's much better than simply thinking well of yourself because you've never fallen on (tested) your gear.

> *. . . then it'll just be a question of how much you want it to hurt.*
> —JACK BAUER, 24

Spacing Protection Points

Your first piece of pro should be placed at a height, from the ground, no greater than the distance from which you could safely jump or fall to a landing. Given a choice, the height of the first piece may depend on factors such as whether the landing is rocky, slopes toward or away from the wall, drops off a ledge, or is cactus-laden—or whether it's pillowy-soft and obstacle-free. Don't count on the latter.

Sometimes, however, you can't place the first piece where you'd like, but instead must put it where the rock allows. This could mean that the leader must climb higher than preferred to place gear. If that's you, then you must assess the risk for yourself and decide whether to proceed with the planned ascent. After all, it's your health that's at stake.

The first piece of gear protects the leader and also helps protect the belayer. As leader, you must consider this simple formula: When you're above the closest piece of gear, you'll fall more than twice as far as the distance from harness waist to that gear. Factors that lengthen the fall include rope stretch and slack in the belay system.

*Kirk Billings safely spaces gear on **Dos Hermanos** (5.12a), Indian Creek.*

What Is Rope Stretch?

Dynamic elongation of rope is measured using the EN892 guidelines. In accordance with this guideline, the following testing regime is carried out. Twenty-eight hundred millimeters (9.2 feet) of rope is attached to an eighty-kilogram weight (176 pounds, simulating the average weight of a climber) from a bollard-and-clamp assembly. The rope is passed through a pivot edge (simulating a carabiner in this example). The weight is raised to a height of 2,300 millimeters (7.5 feet) above this pivot edge and then released. The peak extension is recorded. This is the point where the weight bottoms out. If the peak extension is 3,500 millimeters and the original length was 2,800 mm, the dynamic elongation would be 25 percent. The test is based on a 1.71 factor fall.

To meet EN892 guidelines, only this test for dynamic elongation is mandated. The following information is speculation based on one manufacturer's experience. Thanks to New England Ropes for providing the information that forms the basis of the following paragraphs.

Numerous variables factor into real-world elongation. The full scope of these variables and applications is beyond the scope of this book, but the major ones are discussed below.

One variable is the force of the climber due to accelerated mass under gravitational pull. A second is the angle of each point of protection in a given span. The angle of the rope through the protection plays a significant role in overall elongation, largely because of its effect on fiber reactions and interactions. A third is the length of the fall. A fourth involves the total amount of rope that is out. Others include, but are not limited to, how much rope has been fed out between the gear, the number of protection points, all other points of friction on the rope, the age of the rope, its sheath condition, the number of falls, and all other forms of previous usage. There is no single formula that can encompass all possible variables.

The belay system is also a key factor. Belay considerations include the belayer's position relative to the first piece of gear, whether the belayer is anchored or unanchored, and whether the belay device is connected directly to the anchor or not. Still more variables are the type of belay device used, the reaction time of the belayer, and whether the rope-and-belay system is slack or taut.

A conservative way to look at the advertised elongation is as a worst-case scenario. According to a source from MIT who has worked with the Union Internationale des Associations d'Alpinisme (UIAA, aka International Mountaineering and Climbing Federation), in real-life climbing adventures there is no exact calculation to precisely predict dynamic elongation. "Estimation is possible and useful, but exact calculation is not possible" because of too many variables, unlike the controlled test environment.

A betting man would wager that most climbers would never get the full 28 percent stretch out of their ropes. Remember, the elongation percentage rating is based on a 1.71 factor fall test for UIAA purposes. To exemplify the difficulty in generating such a large factor fall, let's look at simpler math. If a leader who is out 10 feet above the belay on a multipitch route falls, the resulting fall distance would be 20 feet straight onto the belay, making it a factor 2 fall. Fall length divided by the number of feet of rope out from belay device to the leader equals the fall factor. The maximum fall factor is 2. Climbing single-pitch routes reduces the rated fall factors to less than 1, therefore reducing the elongation rating on a rope's hangtag by up to 80 percent.

Generally speaking, the more rope that's out between the belayer and the leader, the greater the rope stretch will be. The average rating of dynamic elongation for spankin'-new premium lead ropes ranges from 26 to 29 percent, but some are even higher. The UIAA permits up to 40 percent elongation for dynamic lead ropes.

The following discussion will assume that a 176-pound leader is climbing a vertical route with a flat landing, with good gear in solid rock and using a rope with a rated elongation of 28 percent that's fed through an anchored belay point, controlled by an attentive belayer. This discussion will accommodate a worst-case scenario, measuring nearly the full 28 percent rope stretch. Please remember that the UIAA permits up to 40 percent elongation for dynamic lead ropes.

If you, as leader, have placed the first gear 10 feet above the ground, climb so that the waist of the harness is 4 feet above that gear, and then fall, the distance of the fall will be 8 feet plus rope stretch—more if your belayer has any slack in the belay system (figure 1). This fall, plus rope stretch, plus slack, would quickly reposition you so that your harness waist would be a realistic minimum of 5 feet below the gear and therefore a maximum of 5 feet above the ground. Also consider that your feet are approximately 3 feet below the harness waist. If you happen to flip upside down, your upper body, head, and arms would occupy the 3 feet normally allotted to your lower limbs. By that

Lead Fall Length Comparison

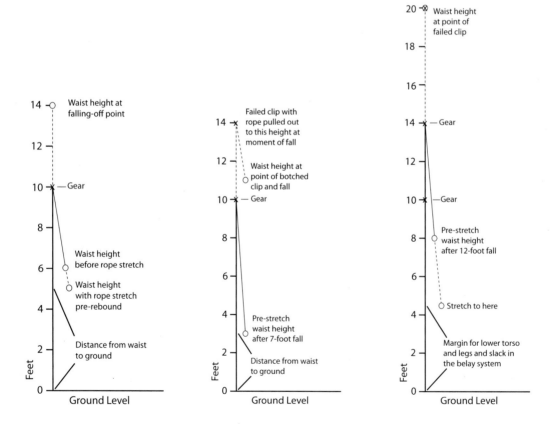

Figure 1

14 –○ Waist height at falling-off point

12 –

10 –✗ —Gear

8 –

6 – ○ Waist height before rope stretch

○ Waist height with rope stretch pre-rebound

4 –

2 – Distance from waist to ground

Feet

0 –
Ground Level

Figure 2

14 –✗ Failed clip with rope pulled out to this height at moment of fall

12 – ○ Waist height at point of botched clip and fall

10 –✗ — Gear

8 –

6 –

4 – ○ Pre-stretch waist height after 7-foot fall

2 – Distance from waist to ground

Feet

0 –
Ground Level

Figure 3

20 –⊗ Waist height at point of failed clip

18 –

16 –

14 –✗ —Gear

12 –

10 –✗ —Gear

8 – ○ Pre-stretch waist height after 12-foot fall

6 –

4 – ○ Stretch to here

2 – Margin for lower torso and legs and slack in the belay system

Feet

0 –
Ground Level

rationale, your toes or head would be *at best* about 2 feet above the ground when the rope bottoms out at its maximum elongation before rebound.

Your second piece of gear should be placed at a height that will prevent a grounder. Better yet, it should be placed so that it provides fall protection with a safe margin for error. If your first piece of gear is 10 feet from the ground, the second would have to be placed only 4 feet above to minimize the risk of a ground fall. The math for this scenario was described in the previous paragraph. This equation only applies if you clip the second piece without

pulling out slack when the gear is clipped at waist height.

If you place the second piece 4 feet above the first, at an arm's length overhead and while your waist is about 12 inches above the first, you'll have to pull up a loop of rope in order to clip (figure 2). This loop would be about 6 feet of rope; then add the 12 inches to the gear below the waist for a total of 7 feet of rope "out" between the first piece of gear and the knot at the harness waist. If you fell from the clipping position with your arm extended and rope in hand in a failed attempt to clip, the fall

Figure 4

Figure 5

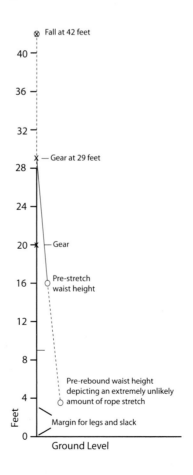

would be at least 14 feet. Your feet would be on the ground even if there were no rope stretch and zero slack in the belay system. For this reason the fall would be lessened and hence safer if you climbed higher and clipped at the waist, without pulling out slack.

Let's now look at what happens when you've progressed up the route and are ready to place your third piece of protection above the second, which was set 14 feet from the ground (figure 3). If you don't mind taking the maximum fall, yet wish to avoid the certainty of grounding out, you can place this third at about 20 feet above the ground, clipping it at waist height, without pulling up rope. A failed clip and fall from this height would give a flight distance of 6 feet to the second piece and continuing another 6 feet to the pre-stretch stopping point; adding 3 feet for the body and toes below the waist leaves a 5-foot margin for rope stretch and belay-system slack. If your actual fall totaled 12 feet, the dynamic rope elongation could be nearly 3½ feet.

Continuing in this vein, your fourth piece could be spaced to a height of 29 feet above the ground (figure 4). A fall from 29 feet with your waist at the gear, but the gear unclipped, would thrill you with an 18-foot ride. Your actual, pre-stretch fall would end 9 feet below the third piece, which is 20 feet above the ground. That 11-foot margin would provide room for 8 feet of potential, albeit unlikely, elongation, a yard from waist to toes, and a belay system with extremely little or no slack.

The fifth piece could be wagered at 42 feet above the ground (figure 5). Failing to clip while the fifth piece is at waist level and falling from there would hand you a 26-foot whipper before rope stretch and give in the belay system. At that moment you'd be 13 feet below the fourth piece and 16 feet above the ground. Subtract an almost impossible maximum of 12½ feet for rope elongation plus 3 feet for your legs, and there remains 6 inches of play. If there's no slack in the belay system and your luck holds, you may scrape by unscathed.

If the sixth piece is placed at the 60-foot mark, clip failure or fall would create a 36-foot screamer, stopping 24 feet above the deck, before elongation. Dynamic elongation, realistically, would be neither 28 percent nor 17 feet. Remember that although a rope under extreme circumstances can elongate up to 28 percent, it is nearly impossible to generate that full a stretch when a rope runs through multiple pieces of gear and a great span (in this case, 60 feet) has been paid out from the belay plate. The remainder would be more than 7 feet to accommodate the legs or head and slack in the belay system.

The higher you are on the route, the farther apart gear can safely be spaced. Of course, this is only true if your placements are perfect, the rock is solid enough to support falls, and everything goes according to plan. It may be worth a body's time to commit to memory the old maxim from Robert Burns: "The best-laid schemes o' mice an' men gang aft agley [often go awry]."

An enormous fall may be noninjurious if the gear holds, the belayer does a good job, you don't hit the wall or anything on the way past, and nothing else goes wrong. Of course, common sense dictates that placing gear closer together to avoid such long falls would be a better choice.

Generally speaking, gear should be placed at regular intervals. When learning to lead, it's smart to place protection no more than 10 to 15 feet apart, even high on a route, for gear that is 2-inch size and larger. The more diminutive the gear, the more closely it should be spaced. For example, ½-inch-size and smaller pieces may be prudently placed a mere 5 feet apart for security.

Small cams have less range on their lobes, and so they can take less movement from their original placement. Improper placement, flaring or marginal placement options, rock breakage, excessive rope drag, or forced movement from being kicked could cause cam movement. Thus it is a good idea to place small cams closer together than larger cams.

Larger nuts tend to be stronger than smaller ones. This is mainly due to the larger size of the cable on which they're swaged. Smaller nuts have less surface area than their larger counterparts, and

The quality of rock should be considered when spacing gear. On soft sandstone like this, many small cams are placed a body length apart. BRIAN BAILEY

More About Placing Protection

An American Climber in Britain

British climbers love a good story. The problem is, to Brits, the only good climbing stories end with hospitalization or death!

Once while climbing on England's gritstone, I was pointed to a classic route by my British host. The route was fairly difficult and gear placements were sparse, but knowing that the route was well within my ability level, up I went, placing gear at each opportunity.

I reached a point about 25 feet up and unexpectedly popped off while placing pro. Down I sailed to the deck, where I made a huge clunk and the rack made a loud clatter. As the rope recoiled from its elongation, it lifted me up and skidded me across the sloping ground until I slammed into the wall. The audio and the visual were dramatic.

A couple of British climbers squealed with anticipation as they scampered over to inquire about how badly I was hurt and how hard I'd hit the ground. I replied that I hadn't actually hit the ground; the rope caught me just as the gear hanging from my harness struck, and that gear had made most of the noise as I was scraping along the landing zone. I wasn't hurt at all. The bewildered Brits could only utter a disappointed "Oh" as they slunk away.

—Steve Petro

Moon Crack *(5.12) is a classic crack on England's gritstone.*

so they're less forgiving if pulled into even a slightly different spot. As with cams, smaller nuts should be placed closer together than larger ones. Some tiny nuts and cams are not made to hold a lead fall; they're intended for aid climbing only. It's good to be aware of the rated strength of each piece of gear on your lead rack.

Choosing a Placement

So where in a crack should you place your well-spaced gear? Let's touch on a few basic types of features and how to protect them.

Because of the shape of the rock, it may not be possible to choose a placement based on distance from the last piece alone. Some cracks are discontinuous, starting and stopping with spans in between. Thus, sometimes the leader places gear where the crack will take it rather than where it wants to go. Some cracks have sections that are too thin or too shallow to take gear. Some sections on a crack may be too flaring to hold gear or too wide for anything on your rack. Maybe you've already used up all the gear that would fit the current placement. There are a multitude of reasons why gear may not fit the crack at a desired interval.

Leading can be scary. If you get frightened on

lead, you may place more gear than safety requires, eventually robbing you of precious stamina. Then you get pumped (rock-hard useless forearms and no grip strength left) and fall, or give up and yell something like "take" or "falling." Since cracks come in so many sizes and shapes—V-slot constriction, mildly undulating, parallel, flaring—effective leading is a skill that takes time to develop. Still, it's a very enjoyable and challenging learning process.

Before leaving the ground, it's important to look up at the route, plan your course, and spot likely locations to stop and place gear. While climbing, it's also important to know where and when to pause for protection placement. It's best to look for relatively easy sections so that sorting through your rack, choosing the correct size, placing the pro in the crack for the best configuration, and then clipping the rope can all be accomplished without error. Set a goal of selecting the correct size every time. This may seem impossible at first, but with continued practice it becomes automatic to lead every pitch choosing the ideal-size pro for each placement. Naturally, you want to avoid dropping a piece, taking too much time to pick out the correct size, or falling while clipping the rope if you're leading. Spying ahead helps you conserve the appropriate-size gear on your rack, and to see the next site to stop and place more gear. The same concept applies when chalking up: Chalk in the easier sections, then climb quickly through the difficult sections. Sometimes you can see that the remainder of the pitch will not require a certain size of protection. If you can use that gear at your current position, it could be advantageous to place it, thus lightening the load for the remainder of your lead. Experience and time spent leading on a regular schedule are two ingredients to develop the necessary skills for leading cracks efficiently, with a cool head.

V-SLOTS

A constriction where the rock necks down to form a V provides perfect placement potential for nuts and hexes. Cams may not seat as well in widely angled V-slots as nuts or hexes. Nuts were made specifically to settle into V-slots and other, lesser constrictions. Hexes offer a variety of sizes and shapes within each unit. Hexes often fill oddly shaped or widely angled spots with ease and efficiency beyond other types of gear.

In a V-slot, cam lobes on an active camming device may not fit well into wide V-shapes. This is because the bottom cams may be fully retracted to fit as tightly as possible, but the upper cam lobes may be too far open for security. Such a device may be unstable and may try to tip out of or walk from its original placement. If a cam moves, it's usually to a worse, less stable placement rather than to a better one.

If the route wanders a bit, consider placing a quickdraw on the wired nut or slung hex to prevent rope drag. Place the nut, give it a small tug, clip the rope, and you are a happy leader doing what you love, climbing upward. The rock may actually bite the wedge because rock is harder than your aluminum nut, keeping it from rotating out as you climb past.

Devils Tower climbs provide an abundance of perfect V-slots for confidence-building nut and hex placements.

SUBTLE CONSTRICTIONS AND UNDULATING CRACKS

A slightly undulating crack offers more challenging nut, hex, and cam placements than a V-slot constriction. *To undulate* means "to move or appear to move in a wavelike manner." Protection slots in undulating cracks are subtle. Non-obvious constrictions litter these cracks, creating a challenge in seeing the protection spot—even when it's right in front of you. Many cracks possess this wavy characteristic, opposed to the acute angles that create V-slots. Wavy constrictions are one specific place where a curved nut almost always works better than a straight-sided one.

If you're leading on an undulating crack climb, you may find that more than one size or genre of gear can fit the same spot. Subtle constrictions might also offer a cam or hex placement. It's good to have options, right? Unless, of course, you

This hex is placed in a subtle constriction in an undulating crack.

depending on its depth. This may be a nice choice if you need to give your fingers or hands a temporary break. It also provides an option for protection location. If, for example, a size 1 Friend fits well deeper in the flare, and out toward the edge a size 2 Friend fits well, you have a choice—which can be very handy, especially if the number of pieces left on your rack is limited.

A cam would be the standard protection device in an outward-flaring crack rather than a nut. Given the way cams expand via spring-loaded lobes, they generally offer greater security in flaring cracks than do nuts or hexes. The two inner cams can be squeezed into a smaller spot than the two outer ones. The beauty of cams is that each pair can expand or contract separately from the other, providing adaptability to many shapes and sizes of cracks. Flaring cracks, found abundantly in Vedauwoo, also offer V-slots with super nut placements.

Sometimes the best spot for gear placement in a flaring crack is exactly where you'd like to jam your hand. This can leave you conflicted about whether to jam or fill the spot with gear instead. If

becomes paralyzed with indecision, confused by too many choices, and end up pumped. Remember that Father Time has a stopwatch on the leader. The time you have to lead a pitch in good style—without falling—is often limited to ten to forty minutes; then you run out of gas. At that point the action may change very quickly from climbing to hanging.

FLARING CRACKS

Flaring cracks are a bit challenging to jam, and tricky to protect as well. An outward-flaring crack is one that becomes wider as it approaches the outside edge of the crack. The deeper you reach into the flaring crack, the narrower it becomes. This narrowing recess can provide a finger jam beyond what may have been a hand jam or even a fist jam,

In a flaring crack two tight cams and two loose ones are often placed. A well-placed cam in this configuration can be very stable. If it's not well placed or gets dislodged, however, it may become useless.

An outward-flaring crack becomes wider as it approaches the outside edge. Here, a climber gropes for flaring jams on **Welzenbach Ged. Weg (5.12d)**, *Röthelfels, Frankenjura.* ULI LENK

only one shallow opening in the crack exists, then you must choose between a secure jam and secure gear placement. Make your choice, live with it rather than whine about the sacrifice, and climb on to the next rest, the next protection spot, or the end of the pitch.

Upon further inspection, however, it's common to discover additional gear-placement spots that weren't obvious at first glance. When a V-slot appears in the back of a flaring crack, it may be possible to place a nut or a small cam in the narrow, back part of the crack, thereby saving the initial spot closer to the outside of the crack for a finger or hand jam. Gear placed deep in a flare should have an extension sling attached to it, to avoid rope drag. The carabiner through which the

rope is clipped should be well outside the crack when the sling is extended. As we've noted, rope drag causes problems by making the rope difficult or even impossible to pull. Drag can also pull gear from its placement.

Sometimes cracks flare inward, opening wider as they recede. The deeper you reach into the crack, the wider the jam, and the bigger the gear that you can place. Take care, though, because it's unlikely that the pro will provide the security you want—and it may become unrecoverable from the abyss. Cams are prone to walking deeper and deeper into the flare, becoming worthless or irretrievable. Hexes and nuts are probably your best bet for inward-flaring cracks.

To place a nut or a hex in an inward flare, find

The climber works for a finger jam in the back of a flare. DAWN KISH

a wider spot on the outer edge of the crack relative to the crack in the vicinity below. Insert the pro into the wide spot and thread it down a little. Then pull it forward, toward the edge of the crack. Gear selected to suit a particular spot in the crack will be too large to pull all the way through to the crack's opening. It should be seated and securely lodged to take a downward, outward pull.

It can be helpful for the leader to yell down to the climber who will clean the route, describing briefly how the gear was placed. The trickier and more circuitous was the gear's path to its placement, the more helpful hints on removal will be. The cleaner removes the gear by reversing its path of entry.

PODS

Pods are circular or elliptical sections on cracks that provide, for example, the much-needed hand jam in a continuous finger crack. Once the pod is vacated by the hand jam, it may be the ideal place in which to set protection. A body length later, this former hand jam morphs into a foot jam, if the gear's not in the way.

Pods can be so small that only your fingertips fit, or they can be large enough to accommodate a knee bar. Some may even be large enough to accommodate a scrunched-up body. This body pod provides a high-probability resting spot—depending, of course, on the size of your body! Pods in cracks usually offer pro spots at the bottom, the top, and somewhere in the back. If you do place pro in the back of the pod, add an extension sling to avoid potential rope drag.

PARALLEL-SIDED CRACKS

Hands-down, the best protection tools for parallel-sided cracks are camming units. To place cams, pull the trigger bar with your forefinger and middle finger, and use your palm or the thumb to push against the end of the stem. Insert the unit and release the trigger bar. Springs pull the cams open, creating pressure against the two sides of the crack. Because of the spiral shape of cam lobes, the harder the pull, the greater the outward pressure on the

This cam is placed on the tightest half of the lobe range. That's a good placement.

unit. As force is applied to the stem, the lobes try to rotate on the axis to provide greater, more powerful contact with the rock.

Nuts and hexes can be nearly impossible to place in parallel-sided cracks. If you do use them, they can be easily dislodged and sent tinkering down the inside of the crack like pinballs bouncing through a slot.

Cams are fast to place, on the other hand, and work like a charm in parallel cracks. They offer an abundance of security—unless they're placed haphazardly or rotate when a careless climber moves past. Because Friends were the first cams on the market, we came up with a motto: *If you kick your Friends, they'll turn on you.* The point is this—and please memorize: A well-placed and secure cam has

A cam that's "tipped out" (too open) like this is a bad placement.

A cam placement is bad if only three out of four cam lobes make contact with the rock.

its stem pointed down toward the ground, not out horizontally (unless it's buried deep in a horizontal placement, of course) and not toward the sky (unless it's set to take an upward pull). The easiest way to compromise an otherwise well-placed cam is to rotate the unit when moving past it. If you don't pay close attention to this detail, you may unwittingly pull a cam from the crack upon falling, not realizing it rotated when you climbed past it.

Excellent climbers watch their feet to make precise foot placements. At no time is this more important than when your feet are moving past a placed camming unit. Your foot must not touch a placed cam or it will nearly always rotate. A very small amount of rotation can be tolerated if the cams do not walk to a wider spot in the crack. But—and here is the Achilles' heel for all spring-loaded cams—if they're rotated too much, they become completely and utterly useless.

If you think of the outer edge of a cam lobe as comprising thirds, then the tightest and the middle third of that surface provides the most secure placement. This middle third of the lobe's outer edge is the area that provides the easiest placement and removal. When the camming device's spring is pulled completely and then placed, the device can become very difficult indeed to remove.

To remove a camming device, the spring must be activated more than it already is in order to retract the cams. The trigger and the lobes must have some play left in their system for additional retraction. Making rock contact on the tightest third of the cam lobe will provide great security, but the lobes may be too retracted to remove. The outer third of the cam lobe edge is a dubious area. In granite a camming device placed open, with rock

Gear placements behind thin flakes can be marginal or bad, since a fall can cause the flake to vibrate, expand, or break.

contact on the outer third of the lobes, can provide a degree of security—*if* no rotation occurs, the lobes do not walk or move at all, and the rock is completely solid. Do not trust an open cam placed on the loosest third of its lobes in soft rock. In the soft, friable sandstone of Indian Creek, for example, the outer third provides only phantom security. Keep in mind that some place out there on the outer third of the cam lobe edge is no security, and eventually no camming action whatsoever. There is no need to test your luck with open cams. If a cam is opened too widely, simply remove it from the crack and start over by pulling the next larger size from your rack instead.

FLAKES

Flakes can be pancake-thin or bread-loaf-thick. Gear placements in thin flakes are difficult to trust, since a fall can cause the flake to vibrate and expand or to break. The flake's movement can easily result in a pulled nut, even if it looked textbook-perfect when first placed. If a thin-flake section is short, consider climbing past the flake before protecting the lead again. Occasionally, there might be protection bolts in the solid rock beside the thin flake. Remember to take a couple of quickdraws if there are bolts to be clipped. Friends will usually work better in flakes than nuts. Camming devices can expand as a flake expands in the event of a fall. Protection inside flakes is a risky business compared with most other rock features.

HORIZONTAL CRACKS

Horizontal cracks can be straightforward when it comes to cam or nut placement. If you're placing a cam in a horizontal, the safest choice by far is a flexible-stemmed unit. If you're forced to put a rigid-stemmed unit in a horizontal, try to place it so an inch or less of the stem lies over the edge. If it *must* stick out over the horizontal edge, it may be possible to avoid leverage on the stem by tying it off short, closer to the cams. This technique, known as the Gunks tie-off, is illustrated on the Wild Country Web site (www.wildcountry.co.uk).

Placing nuts in horizontal constrictions can be

Horizontal cracks require flexible-stemmed cams, because rigid stems might break on the edge.

devious and may require two nuts used in combination: one to the right, one to the left, connected with one or two slings to set the proper direction of pull in the event of a fall. Two extension slings rather than one may be required to reduce or eliminate potential rope drag.

It's fairly unusual to find more than one horizontal crack on a pitch unless you're climbing at the Gunks or on southern sandstone. Sometimes horizontal cracks are found in the back of ledges or at the end of pitches on multipitch routes.

DIAGONAL CRACKS

Cracks usually run vertically, and are occasionally cut by a horizontal crack. Cracks that run diagonally up and left or up and right, though a bit rare to find, offer some of the best crack climbing around. Maybe the reason they're so much fun is that they seem a bit unusual. Some of our own favorite cracks of all time are diagonally oriented: *Sphinx Crack* in Colorado; *The Phoenix, Equinox, Rubicon, Illusion Dweller,* and *Do or Fly* in California; *Fallen Arches* and *Mexican Crack* in Utah; and the *Diagonal* in Wyoming, to name a few.

Climbing diagonal cracks usually requires that one foot is always in the crack while the other is frequently out on the face.

Diagonal cracks require special attention: It's easier to dislodge a nut when you're moving past, because the wired nut isn't pointed straight down in the most secure configuration. Since you may be shuffling finger or hand jams on lead, as opposed to crossing through, placing gear between your waist and chest is better than above your head. This avoids the problem of the gear getting in the way of your higher hand when you're moving a hand (especially the upper one) to the next jam. Normally, the lower hand jams thumbs-up while you place gear with your upper hand in a diagonal crack. If you're placing pro with your lower hand, you'd normally jam your upper hand thumbs-down.

Special Placements and Considerations

Now that you know the basics of placing and spacing gear, and what rock features to place it in, let's look at few more advanced considerations.

Directionals

A directional is a piece of gear placed to direct the path of the rope or the path of force in the event of a fall. Becoming familiar with some of the most common uses for directionals is an important step toward a safe system and a happy journey.

A directional may divert the rope's path away from a dangerously sharp edge or away from features that might cause rope drag. Directional gear

Climbing diagonal cracks like this may require one foot to be always in the crack while the other is frequently out on the face. Here, Lisa Gnade climbs Sphinx Crack (5.13c and created by an explosion!).
BRIAN BAILEY

More About Placing Protection

can also keep the rope running in a path that keeps it from getting stuck in a crack, a bush, or some other place you don't want it to go.

A directional may protect the leader in case of fall by keeping the force on other pieces of gear in desired orientation. We'll describe a specific example of this in the upcoming section "Upward Directionals."

Directional gear can also offer protection by controlling where you'll land at the end of a fall, if you're leading. It could direct you safely away from a protrusion of some sort—say, an arête, corner, ledge, block, or tree. A directional can prevent you from falling or swinging into a spot from which it may prove difficult to get back onto the route.

When a route traverses or is overhanging, you might place a piece of gear as a courtesy for the person who will follow or second the pitch, regardless of whether or not you think it necessary to protect the lead. This gear would protect the second/follower in the event of a fall, especially from swinging into a void, blank, or difficult section of wall and out of reach of the route. It could also direct the second away from a potentially injurious situation.

Protect the belayer on a multipitch route by directing force from a lead fall to a comfortable and safe spot for the belayer; you want to make sure that the force of any fall you take doesn't pull directly on him or her. Your force or weight should

The directional on this multipitch would direct the force of a falling leader onto the gear, rather than straight onto the belayer. KLAUS FENGLER/RED CHILI

instead be directed onto gear first. Also take care to set up a directional that ensures you can't hit the belayer or the belay station during a fall.

On multipitch routes, if a belayer is above, bringing up the second who is below, creating an upward pull on the belayer through an anchor point that is above him or her will provide comfort and safety. If the second hangs, the biner that's clipped onto the overhead directional will act like a passive pulley of sorts, reducing the pull on the belayer. It's more comfortable for the belayer to have an upward pull on the harness—that's the pull direction for which harnesses are designed. Create an upward directional pull so the belayer's hips are not getting crushed by a downward pull from a dangling climber. It will be less strenuous on the belayer and will provide greater mobility for adjustments.

Upward Directionals

Typically, all the gear placed in a crack is expected to hold a downward force in the event of a fall. Sometimes, however, the leader's first gear placement will act as an upward directional. This means that the first piece is actually placed upside down from the standard orientation. Gear set as an upward directional will hold an upward pull.

The reason for placing an upward directional, especially as the first piece of gear on a route, is to provide or maintain a downward pull on the pro above. This is especially important if the next pro is a wired nut. If the belayer's stance is away from the wall, the rope runs from the belay plate, bending around the biner on the first piece of gear and then continuing up at a different angle to the leader or gear above. This change of angle creates friction, aka rope drag. Even if the belayer's stance is close

Here, the lower cam acts as an upward directional for the upper cam.

The lower nut is set as an upward directional for the upper nut.

to the wall, as the leader climbs up past the first piece of gear, the rope drags and lifts the carabiner that's attached to the protection or its sling. If the gear were placed in a standard orientation to take only a downward pull, the upward pull from the rope could lift a nut from its intended orientation or cause a cam to rotate or walk from its original placement. If the upward lift is hard enough, it might force the gear to pop from the placement and fall out of the rock completely.

If a line of nuts has been placed to take downward force only, it's possible to zipper all the gear from the route, especially during a fall. The term *zipper* refers to the unintended high-speed ripping of multiple pieces of gear—sometimes all of it—from a crack in successive order. This happens most commonly when a leader has not placed an upward directional as the lowest piece, and all gear above is set for a downward pull only. If the leader falls, the rope drag pulls up on the first piece, lifting it out of placement. If the first piece pops, then the rope drag pulls up on the second piece as the leader plunges downward. If the second piece rips up and out, then the rope lifts up on the third piece, while the leader falls farther . . . and so on and so forth, until eventually the force may pop the top piece out of placement, essentially cleaning the route of gear. Of course, the final result is a grounder.

It's possible to zipper all your gear without falling just by upward-pulling rope drag while you climb. If you look down at your feet while leading and notice that all your pro has fallen out of the crack and is dangling from the rope, you may find a lump in your throat and a puddle in your shoe.

It's best to plan for an upward pull on the first piece of gear before starting up a pitch, because once you're up a couple body lengths, correcting the error may be precarious.

Two protection pieces are equalized by a sling to share the load in case of a fall.

Doubling Up

If the route to the next piece looks really run-out, the leader may choose to double up on pieces, placing them very close together. Doubling up might also save the day if the next higher placement, after the run-out, were to rip during a fall. Putting two pieces in close proximity may be an emotionally reassuring tactic. Naturally, this may be redundant if the current piece is bomber (placed so well that King Kong would not rip it in a fall), and it may

Dunked in Fremont Canyon

One day in Fremont Canyon, Wyoming, we watched our friend Scott Carson lead the crack *Short 'n' Sassy*. From the opposite side of the canyon, we could witness every move and gear placement with a bird's-eye view. From the belay ledge, the route traverses right, over the river and out of sight of the belayer. It then turns upward, ascending a finger crack to the rim of the canyon.

Scott had been climbing well and had recently developed a certain taste for running routes out. Only the day before, he had successfully performed his most daring lead yet, on sparsely placed gear. He was emboldened by the experience. Achieving a new level of success by breaking through previous self-imposed mental or physical barriers sometimes leaves a climber with a sense of invincibility. It's like having newly granted superpowers.

Scott screwed his cap tightly onto his head and left the belay ledge with rack and courage, disappearing from the belayer's view. He climbed confidently, placing gear in all the best spots, all the while being cajoled and receiving kudos from the peanut gallery.

When he was about 25 feet out, Scott placed his third piece, a bomber textbook-perfect nut, and attached it to the rope with a quickdraw. The nut was so good that it inspired confidence, even when the next possible placement proved so thin that it would hold only a tiny brass wire.

A climber raps in to climb during a typical day in Fremont Canyon.

Tiny brass wires are useful, but are rated for aid, not for taking lead falls. Scott considered climbing back down and doubling up gear by the nut where there were placement options. The nut was so good, however, and he felt strong, so the risk appeared minimal. He decided to proceed rather than waste time and energy climbing back down to place redundant gear.

A little higher, the crack turns sassy and features a shallow, bottoming flare. This was the only place for Scott to put gear, and the only piece he had that would fit the flare was a three-cam unit. The crack is very shallow there, so instead of placing a well-fitting unit as he'd hoped, Scott managed only to engage two of the three cams. The cam looked sketchy—and he knew that the brass wire would not hold a hard fall—so he again considered climbing back down to the bomber nut to back it up. But no, that nut was just too good. And it was far enough from the deck to keep him from hitting, even in the unlikely event of the other two pieces pulling.

So up he went. Scott's belayer kept ample slack in the system to keep the rope from pulling on him as he continued.

He reached an awkward mantle from which he could reach up and clip the anchor. The loud cheers turned to congratulations . . . just as his foot slipped off the hold. Down he went. Out popped the malcontent cam and down went Scott even farther. Then the brass nut deformed

(continued on page 92)

(continued from page 91)

to a useless little chunk and went sailing down with him until they reached the bomber nut. The nut held. The quickdraw, however, disassembled itself so that one biner and the sling stayed attached to the nut, but the other biner came off the sling and stayed on the rope. Needless to say, down went Scott.

The crowd of onlookers fell dead-silent as he hit the watery deck and disappeared among the boulders lurking below the Fremont River's surface. Seconds passed, wide eyes searched, and minds raced. Just as we were about to leap to the rescue, a baseball cap popped out of the water, with an intact head and a big goofy grin attached. "I'm fine," Scott called, and the silence was broken by hysterical laughter.

In America the best stories have happy endings and tell of lessons learned.

drain the leader of energy needed to continue on the route.

Being run out is one reason to double up on gear. Another occurs if one piece of gear is marginal—but perhaps it's fitted into the best or only place to put it. As soon as the option presents itself, it's appropriate to throw in an additional piece, especially a well-seated nut or cam.

Sometimes you simply feel the need for protection. Go ahead and place it. But once you're safely on the ground, think back and reassess. Ask, *Did I really need to spend time and stamina there to place extra pro, or was the climb completely safe at that point? Was I irrationally prompted to overprotect the pitch?* Any aspiring leader must ask many such questions, analyzing every decision made in order to eliminate errors and minimize mistakes. A chain is only as strong as its weakest link.

Is a marginal piece worth spending time and strength to place if, only a few moves higher, there may be a bomber placement? What if the bomber placement, as viewed from below, was actually an optical illusion offering no protection placements once you'd already climbed to it? Or what if the illusion misled you into thinking the appropriate piece of gear was on your rack—only to find that a different size was needed, but not available? And what if the previous marginal but potential gear wasn't placed? These are some of the questions a lead climber must anticipate.

Sometimes, or even most of the time, right or wrong answers do not exist. You make the best choices you can given the circumstances, and then move to the next set of choices, repeating the process continually until the climb is finished. As P.T. Barnum said, "You pays your money and you takes your chances." Rock climbing is a risky activity, and you're responsible for your own choices whether you accept it or not. Wherein Mr. Barnum added, "Facts do not cease to exist because they are ignored."

Avoiding Rope Drag

Routes that meander, roofs, and double-crack systems all create the unsavory opportunity to die in drag. Rope drag is created by friction and causes the rope to feel abnormally heavy. It happens when the rope changes angles or rubs across a rough surface. There may be so much friction from gear and rock that it can be extremely difficult, even impossible to pull the rope up in order to clip it. If you're leading, you're well advised to look down the route before clipping each piece of gear, to make sure the rope's line is running as straight as possible. Extensions such as runners or long slings should be applied when appropriate to help alleviate friction-causing crooks in the rope. If you look down and see the rope making sharp angles as it runs from your belayer through the various protection placements, it's almost certainly dragging on you like a weight around your waist. No exaggeration, rope drag can stop you dead in your tracks. Hopefully it's not too

Extension runners are placed on gear to reduce rope drag by straightening the path of the rope.

An extension draw is added to straighten the rope's line.

then climb down to the next piece until you reach the point where the rope's path is straight. On your way back up the route, each piece of gear may need an extension runner to avoid a repetition of the mistake. This method would involve downleading the route and then releading it back up.

Alternatively, you might be able to downclimb past clipped gear without weighting the rope, adding longer slings to the gear as you pass. This way, instead of downleading, you'd be protected by a toprope while climbing down. Once the rope's path has been sufficiently straightened, you then have toprope protection as you climb back up to the highest point of protection and resume the lead.

We suggest that you, as leader, take at least three to five extra quickdraws and a couple of extra over-the-shoulder slings (60 centimeter) on every trad pitch with changing angles, whether these are lateral or inclination changes. There are exceptions. On some routes in Indian Creek, a leader would seldom need to add a quickdraw to a protection piece because the cracks form very straight lines with minimal or no angle changes. In Utah's Little Cottonwood Canyon, on the other hand, some multipitch routes meander so much that two or three over-the-shoulder slings are a bare minimum. Another reason to bring a few extra long slings is that sometimes you encounter natural pro such as a small tree trunk around which a sling can be wrapped; long slings come in handy for this.

You can also avoid rope drag by not overprotecting the crack. Overprotecting means placing more gear than is necessary to safely lead the climb. It can cause great discomfort on lead by creating rope drag. It can also cause you to run out of strength or to become pumped from hanging on too long as you place exorbitant amounts of gear. The goal, of course, is to finish the climb safely and in good style—without falling. Place enough gear to be safe, but if the gear is solid, don't overdo it.

Routes in England and Wales often require protecting discontinuous cracks that wander and act like a double-crack system. Alpine and British climbers have learned to use two ropes to deal, in part, with the issue of rope drag. The two-rope sys-

late when you notice that you've got rope drag in the system, and you can continue to the end of the pitch.

If the drag has become unbearable, the popular choice is to climb down to the highest piece. Once you're there, you have a couple of options. One is to instruct your belayer to "take" and to "lower." As you're being lowered, add quickdraws (10 to 15 centimeters, like those used for sport climbs) and runners (30-, 60-, or 120-centimeter sewn slings) to straighten the rope's path through the carabiners.

The other way to correct the problem of rope drag is to downlead without weighting the rope. To do this, unclip each piece of pro in succession and

tem entails, for example, using one rope to clip pieces on the your left and a different-colored rope to clip pieces on your right. The two different-colored ropes are 8 to 9 millimeters in diameter, and the system is called the double-rope technique. This can be a rather confusing system, especially at first. The neophyte double-rope leader has to remember whether to clip the red rope or the blue rope to the right-hand piece. And of course, what if you've accidentally crossed the ropes, ironically creating rope drag, the very thing the system is intended to prevent? Although it may seem inconvenient at the moment, you must correct the crossed rope before moving higher or there will be repercussions.

A roof crack can be not only intimidating, but also downright challenging when it comes to preventing rope drag. First, don't place gear in the back of the roof (where it meets the vertical wall). This would result in something close to a 90-degree angle on the rope as it bends and passes over the carabiner, causing severe rope drag. Remember, rope drag is friction from the rope running through biners between you and your belayer. (Of course, rope drag can also be caused by the rope running across the rock.)

Strongly consider placing a 30- or 60-centimeter sling on this last piece before crawling into the roof section of the route. This would replace the 90-degree angle with two oblique ones—say, two 135-degree angles—which would create less friction.

Beyond the last point on the vertical wall, the climbing will become seriously more strenuous. So from this last position before starting the roof, if possible, consider placing another piece of pro about an arm's length out the roof. It's important not to put the gear at such a great arm span that clipping the rope becomes a task. Also, take care not to place gear exactly where a finger or hand, foot or toe jam will need to go. Sometimes placing pro from the last position on the vertical wall may be too difficult, or it may take the only spot for a crucial jam. In this case you must move out under the roof and then place the next protection device.

Proceeding, you'll climb to the roof's outer edge, called the lip, placing gear about every 4 or 5 feet. Placing gear closer than this gets in the way of feet and hands, while situating it farther apart means that if you fall, getting back up to the crack will be very strenuous indeed! In fact, if you fall with gear more than 4 or 5 feet apart, the only way back up to the crack may be to boink.

Boinking, in climber-speak, means grasping the rope and pulling your body up as the belayer pulls against you with all his or her weight. When you let go of the rope, the belayer will jolt lower a few inches to a foot. Then you grasp the rope again and pull up, with the belayer again pulling against you. This tiresome procedure is repeated until you can be boinked back up to the crack. Once you're within reach of the gear, abdominal reprieve, rest, and recovery of breath may be regained by clipping a quickdraw from your harness's belay loop into the pro.

Gear placements within a foot above and below the lip of the roof should generally be avoided. The rope may drag from friction created by the 90-degree angle that the rope would make; the rope can also become pinned between the rock and the pro, causing severe or unbearable rope drag. It's usually better to turn the lip, elevating your torso or even your entire body out from under the roof onto the vertical face above, before placing more pro. When placing gear below and above a roof, carefully consider adding extended runners to the gear to alleviate potential rope drag or binds.

Someone who is comfortable leading 5.10 trad routes may wisely consider leading, at maximum, a 5.9 trad roof for a rewarding first-roof-crack adventure.

Additional Hardware and Necessities

Color-Coded Carabiners

Color-coded carabiners to match cams can be a time-saving device, as well as a joy to behold. Cams are anodized in a color specific to their size. By adding a matching-color carabiner to each cam, you can quickly identify and select the desired cam without rifling through your rack to see which sling is connected to which carabiner. Some racks consist

Using color-coded carabiners makes cam identification fast and easy.

of multiple brands of cams, which may be anodized a different color per brand, per same-size piece. That's another prime candidate for color-coded biners. In such case all pieces fitting a certain size crack—for instance, all 1½-inch cams—can be racked on the same color carabiner for easy size ID, regardless of brand and cam color. After all it's the biner that you actually pull from the rack; the gear is subsequently attached to it.

Locking Carabiners

Locking biners are a staple item for any roped climbing experience. Take at least a couple per person for crack climbing days. One will be used with the belay and rappel device; the other can be used to clip in at anchors. It's better to have an unused extra in the pack than to create unnecessary risk by having too few lockers. Locking carabiners are like chocolates: Why have just one?

Screw-gate-locking carabiners have a manual-style locking mechanism on the gate. This requires you to tighten the spindle by turning it by hand until it's either locked or unlocked, as desired. The ever-popular screw gates are staple items on a trad rack. They can be used with a belay or rappel device, or as attachment points for anchors, trailing ropes, aiders, or other items. They may also add security on gear that's situated so as to cause con-

Take at least two locking biners per person for crack climbing days, especially multipitch. When selecting a belay or rappel device, consider whether the system will need to accommodate one rope or two.

cern that a nonlocking biner may become accidentally unclipped. Screw gates are particularly more adaptable to using in lieu of a nonlocking biner on placed pro than their auto-locking counterparts. This is because they can be racked with the gate in the unlocked orientation and employed easily, like a nonlocking biner. Once it's securely clipped to pro and rope, you can manually lock the biner.

Quicklocks are automatic-locking biners with a two-step mechanism. First, rotate the spindle on the gate. Then push the gate open. Once the gate has been released, it will snap shut and the spindle will automatically spin to the locked position. While auto-locking biners provide enhanced con-

venience for many tasks, they are not especially easy to substitute for nonlockers for quick, one-handed rope clips. Auto-locking carabiners are plenty easy for rapid-fire attachments to gear and other points. However, trying to rotate the spindle with the same hand that's holding a rope up to clip it through the biner provides an unwelcome challenge, because your other hand is unavailable while you're hanging on to a tenuous hold or jam.

Locksafe-locking carabiners are classified as three-step automatic lockers: Lift the spindle, rotate it, and push the gate open. Here again, once the gate is released it will snap shut and the spindle will automatically return to the locked position.

Belay and Rappel Devices

Belay devices come in various forms. They can be as simple as a high-strength chain link or as complicated as an active camming contraption. Whatever the choice, a good belay device is indispensable for a safe, comfortable belay. Additionally, many belay devices can be used for rappelling.

Whether you're belaying or rappelling, consider if the system will need to accommodate one rope or two. If you'll be using two ropes for belaying or rappelling, or using a doubled rope to set up a rap, you need a device like a DMM Bug or a V-Twin or Wild Country VC Pro. These are essentially small, shapely chunks of aluminum or steel featuring two rope slots.

You could also opt for a Figure 8, a classic belay and rappel device named for its shape. The standard Figure 8 has one larger end and one smaller. This allows frictional variation for situational considerations such as thin ropes, thick ropes, single ropes, double ropes, low-angle rappels, free-hanging rappels, rappelling with a heavy load, and more. Although a lot of technology has been developed since the dawn of the Figure 8, it's still hard to beat this old classic, especially for rappels. It's easy to handle, gives a smooth ride, is relatively gentle on the rope, and is long lasting.

As we've mentioned previously, we assume you know the basics of belaying and rappelling. For more information, consult a beginner's manual such as *How to Rock Climb!* by John Long.

Other Gear Necessities

HARNESS

When selecting a harness for crack climbing, keep in mind the large quantity and heavy weight of gear that it will be expected to carry. Four or five generous-size gear loops will certainly come in handy. A given pitch may require twenty pieces of gear for protection. Collectively, the harness's gear loops should have ample room on which to clip at least twenty carabiners, with gear attached. Gear loops should be spaced around the sides and back of the harness. If the loops are too far forward, gear will hang in front of your body, between your legs, in your way. This inhibits movement and leads to maddening readjusting or shoving of gear.

Look for a comfortably padded, well-fitting harness. When fully loaded with gear, the harness will ride lower on your hips and will be quite heavy. Consider the waistband's contour on your body and the amount of padding on pressure points. Leg loops should fit comfortably, too. Leg loops that are too tight can feel restraining and prevent natural movement. If the loops are too loose, on the other hand, they will slide down the back of your thigh, losing their ability to give properly placed support.

Whether a harness has fixed or adjustable leg loops is a matter of personal choice. Some people prefer buckled, adjustable legs, thinking that they will wear the harness over vastly different thickness of clothing during different seasons. Others like the lighter weight and less bulky feeling of fixed leg loops. Most fixed-leg harnesses incorporate a small elastic expansion strap on each leg loop for comfort and to offer a modest range of fit over various layers of clothing.

SHOES

Comfortable shoes with a low toe profile are part of a good starter kit for crack climbing. The term *low toe profile* is a way of describing the height of the toe box, calculated vertically from the bottom of the sole to the top of the toe tip above your big-toe toenail. A low profile will provide a relaxed yet high-performance fit for cracks.

Shoes should fit snugly but not be toe-curling tight. Toes that are slightly bent and firmly packed will feel better when jammed into a crack than toes that are knuckled under and balled up. Worse than discomfort, it's possible that overly scrunched toes may be too bulbous to fit into would-be jams in the first place. Foot jams also grind on the sides of shoes. For increased durability, consider a lined shoe. Lining puts one more layer of material between your foot and the rock; it also adds a slight padding and takes longer to wear through.

Shoes with stiff midsoles are supportive in foot jams and wide cracks. Lace-up shoe models are rec-

A day at the cracks requires an assortment of gear and other necessities.

ommended for jams that go deeper than a toe's length. The lacing system runs on top of the foot, where it's not on a major pressure point or abrasion spot in foot jams. Softer-soled shoes will be more sensitive for narrow cracks and pods in finger cracks. Hook-and-loop closure systems such as Velcro can work well for tiny, straight-in cracks where the foot never enters the crack and never scrapes against the rock. In wider cracks, though, abrasion will quickly eat through hook-and-loop straps or cause them to open. This would be a consumer-choice error, not a manufacturer's defect.

Remember, it's all about selecting the right tool for the job.

Select a harness with plenty of gear loops for crack climbing, keeping in mind the quantity and weight of gear it will be expected to carry.

More About Placing Protection

Shoes with a low-profile toe construction are best for crack climbing. Lace-up shoes are generally preferable when the foot will be jammed deeper than the toes.

> *In the midst of a land without silence you have to make a place for yourself. Those who have worn out their shoes many times know where to step. It is not their shoes you can wear only their footsteps you may follow—if you let it happen.*
>
> —CHIEF DAN GEORGE,
> "WORDS TO A GRANDCHILD"

CHALK BAG

Select a chalk bag that's large enough to easily accommodate a taped hand. Taped hands are cumbersome and less agile than bare hands. It can be annoying and problematic to have a hand become stuck inside the chalk bag. Usually, a relatively large, cylindrical bag is the most convenient shape for crack climbing.

TAPE

Many climbers choose to tape hands and fingers in order to save skin. Although bare skin sticks better to rock than does tape, tape sticks better than bloody pulp. If you've developed sufficient calluses on your hands, tape may not be necessary. Without calluses,

Sometimes nicks happen despite a well-planned tape job. SEBASTIAN SCHWERTNER

taping will boost your confidence, can reduce your chances of injury, and will be appreciated by those who climb the route shortly after you and wish to have at least a semi-hygienic experience.

Use cotton-based athletic tape to wrap joints and other bony spots that are subject to rock rash and flappers (skin ripped loose, exposing bloody underlayers). One roll of tape will probably cover both hands and fingers a couple of times. After climbing, be sure that all tape bits are securely stowed in your backpack's trash compartment.

There are many ways to tape a hand. Just about everyone thinks his or her own way is best. Shown here are a couple of the right ways to tape.

Taping Method 1

1. Start at the pinkie knuckle on the back of the hand.

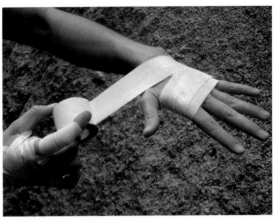

2. Wrap the tape around the hand in unwrinkled, partially overlapping layers, spiraling down the hand to and around the wrist.

3. Leave some slack between the inside of the wrist and the tape so the wrist can flex without binding against the tape, cutting off circulation.

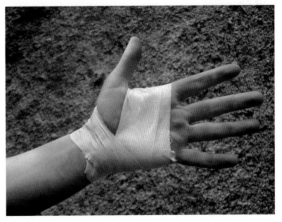

4. This method involves covering both the back and the palm of the hand.

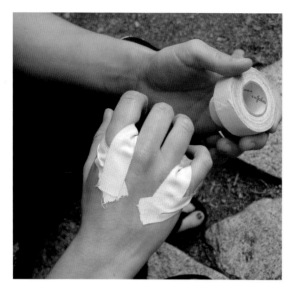

1. *Another way to tape is to cover the back of the hand and leave the palm bare. Begin by tearing off a couple of thin strips of tape. Wrap a strip around the first finger and pat the ends down on the back of the hand. Then wrap the other strip around the little finger and pat the ends down on the back of the hand.*

2. *Tear off one wide strip at a time. The strips should be long enough to cover the back of the hand perpendicular to the fingers while the hand is held in a loosely contracted fist.*

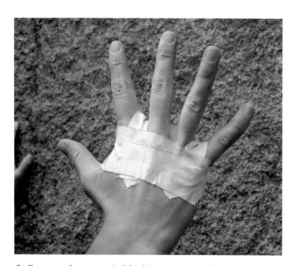

3. *Secure the unwrinkled tape to the skin.*

4. *Repeat process down to the wrist, with edges of strips slightly overlapping.*

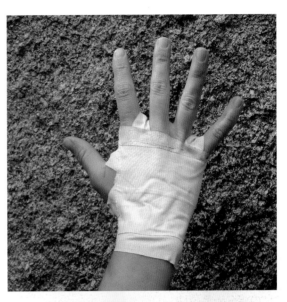

5. Next, place one end of a long, thin strip of tape on the back of the hand, below the fore knuckle. Run the tape down and around the thumb, then back up and across the back of the hand. Continue around to encircle the wrist.

6. Next, apply additional wide strips on the back of the hand to cover the ends of the thin strip. The finished result should be a hand well covered with smooth tape.

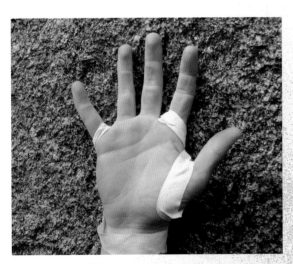

7. The palm will be bare, which increases its sensitivity to the rock.

1. To tape fingers, start as close to the nail as desired and then spiral-wrap the finger to its base.

2. Keep the tape snug and wrinkle-free. It is usually best to hold the fingers in a slightly bent position while taping—this allows the fingers to either straighten or curl with only moderate effort.

ROPES

Bi-pattern ropes are preferred by many climbers. A bi-pattern rope changes pattern at the halfway mark. Bi-patterns are particularly handy for adventure climbing, where you may not know the precise route length ahead of your ascent. When you're approaching the halfway point, the belayer can usually estimate the amount of rope remaining by visually tracing the pile of rope and counting feet before the pattern changes. Later, when setting up a rappel, bi-patterns make finding the midway point a breeze. If you're in doubt whether both ends of the rope have reached the proper stopping point (either the ground or the next anchor), tie a knot in the end of the rope(s)!

The length and diameter of your rope will depend on where you plan to do most of your climbing and also your personal preferences. The most common ropes are 60 to 70 meters long with diameters ranging from 9.5 to 10.2 millimeters. A lot of climbers like "dry" ropes that resist becoming soaked with water.

Bi-pattern ropes change their woven pattern midway.

PART III

Hitting the Crags

Decisions to Make

Where to Go

America is Mecca for crack climbers. There are many thousands of cracks in hundreds of climbing areas across the United States, and innumerable more spread around the globe. Let's assume, for our discussion, that you're looking for a crack climbing paradise within the US. Yosemite, Paradise Forks, Devils Tower, Vedauwoo, Indian Creek, South Platte, and Joshua Tree, to name a modest few, host beloved, classic lines and are renowned worldwide.

The quality and quantity of cracks to climb in these areas could be thought of as icing on the cake. The areas are substantive and awe-inspiring destinations for nonclimbers and climbers alike. Each merits a visit just to experience being in that spot on the planet. Hiking, picnicking, taking photos, relaxing and taking in the scene, or any number of other activities make life in such beautiful places satisfying. Climbing is an added treat.

What to Do

When visiting a new climbing destination, why not start with a comfortably rated, five-star classic to acclimatize to the area?

The area's guidebook should offer lists and descriptions of routes. Such descriptions may include clues as to the nature of the climbing—dihedral, splitter, overhanging, vertical, crimpy face, pockets, tricky, runout, what have you. It may also

Early-morning light in Joshua Tree is as stunning as the routes. BRIAN BAILEY

Campsite King Brian Bailey kicks back with a cooler full of elk bourguignonne.

include gear suggestions and the length of the route. It may state whether a rappel or a walk-off will be required and where to locate the rap station or the walk-down. Each route is rated for difficulty. Most routes are classed between 5.2 (the easier end of the scale) and 5.15 (the current max). The preponderance of routes will fall between 5.6 and 5.12. Most guidebooks offer a star rating to indicate

Utah's Little Cottonwood Canyon offers some classic granite cracks like **Fallen Arches (5.13a).**

PART III: HITTING THE CRAGS

the route's quality. For example, five stars may follow some routes' names. This would indicate the highest quality possible in a five-star rating system. Other routes may get fewer or even no stars. Some routes will be termed "classic," meaning that they embody the spirit of the area's climbing.

When you're arriving at an area that's new to you, it's wise to select a few warm-up routes that are well within your comfort range. Warm-ups let you ease onto an unfamiliar rock type. It may take a few pitches at a new area to gain confidence. Breaking into the grades at a leisurely pace will provide time to adjust to the area's idiosyncrasies. Acclimatizing to rock texture, features, and types of holds and moves; getting a feeling for gear placements; and comparing the area's ratings with grades at other areas are some of the worthy considerations that will enhance your experience. Remember that warming up is as much for the head as it is for the body.

Starting the climbing day gently increases blood circulation and oxygen supply to your muscles. Warming your muscles somewhat gradually helps them function at full capacity, should they be called upon to do so, later in the workout. Muscles that have been properly warmed up have greater endurance and can pull harder than those prematurely subjected to overly pumpy or maximum-strength tasks.

To avoid a mental or physical epic, try a route that meets a very reasonable expectation rather than jumping on the hardest, scariest imaginable route straight off the block. Becoming gripped by fear does not make you climb better. Neither does thrashing, bleeding, pumping out, falling excessively far, falling too many times, ripping gear,

Viewing desert spires in changing light is spectacular. Climbing them is an added treat.

dropping gear, throwing a tantrum, screaming, cursing, soiling yourself, stressing out your belayer, or other sundry misadventures with gravity.

Work to develop an overall sense of comfort and well-being on the rock.

Once you've accrued a good gauge for the routes and an accurate self-assessment, it's time to move on to more ambitious tasks.

> *Near certainty of death, small chance of success, what are we waiting for?*
> —GIMLI,
> FROM *LORD OF THE RINGS* BY J. R. R. TOLKIEN

What to Bring

The question *What do I need to take to the crags?* is best answered by the questions *Where are you going?* and *What are you doing?* To start with, bring the following items:
- Guidebook.
- Gear.
- Rope.
- Other staples such as shoes, harness, slings, daisies, chalk bag, tape, water, helmet if desired, and any other items that you use habitually during a day at the crags.

Guidebook

Guidebooks are indispensable references. They usually provide information about the area, directions and maps, route descriptions and grades, trail-finding info, descent recommendations, topographical drawings and/or elevation views to locate the routes on the walls, photos, discussions of local climbing history, ethical and environmental considerations, camping or where to stay, where to eat, shop, or fuel up, and other useful tidbits.

Once you've selected your destination, a guidebook for the area can help you sort out issues of what you'll need on the routes in general and on each route specifically.

Take the guidebook.

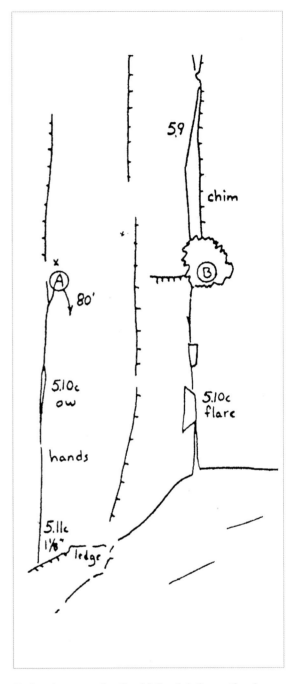

A classic example of guidebook information is found on this page of George Meyers and Don Reid's **Yosemite Climbs.**

When visiting a new destination, start with an area classic such as this multipitch 5.7 on Intersection Rock at Joshua Tree.

A pile of gear models for a still life after a big day at the crag.

Rack

Again, check your guidebook and formulate a plan. Guidebooks help you select routes within your desired difficulty range or grade. Most good ones also provide an indication of what size gear you'll need to lead each route. The gear list in a guidebook is not meant as gospel—merely helpful suggestion. Your individual gear choices or needs may vary from the recommendations given in the guide or from another climber's selected rack.

Below is a list of suggested gear that would make up a minimum standard rack for leading at many traditional/crack climbing areas, especially on granite classics in the Valley or at Joshua Tree. We've also suggested the range of sizes for various sizes of cracks you'll find on a weekend or week-long visit. Of course, you wouldn't take all this gear on every pitch.

- 2 sets of Wallnuts or Rocks sizes 1–10.
- 1 set of Peenuts, Superlight Rocks, or other small offset nuts.
- 2 sets of Friends sizes 00–4.
- Friends sizes 5 and 6, if off-widths are on the menu.

Hey, check out my rack! *A rack full of gear is sure to impress tourists as much today as in yesteryear.*

- 10 quickdraws.
- 15 free biners.
- 4 60-centimeter slings.
- 2 120-centimeter slings.
- 1 belay/rappel device per person.
- 2–3 locking biners per person.
- Nut tool.
- Gear sling (optional).
- Items listed in "Other Staples" below.

If you're headed to Indian Creek, however, take five to ten of each size Friend and no nuts at all. The cracks there tend to be parallel-sided and are therefore very continuous in size. On a specific crack, for example, you may use one to three size 3 Friends, then three to five size 2.5 Friends, then four to six size 2 Friends, then three to five size 1.5 Friends.

Most sandstone is softer than granitic and igneous rock types. Soft sandstone can break easily. This means that for safety's sake, you'll want to place gear close together. As a general rule, the smaller the crack, the closer your gear must be placed. Smaller cams have inherently less lobe range than larger ones. Rock breakage or cam movement could cause gear to pop out of its placement. The smaller the gear, the less forgiving it is of disturbances. Running it out, or climbing far above the last point of gear, is not advised on soft rock, and especially not on finger cracks.

When headed to Devils Tower, it would be wise to take two or three sets of nuts, a set of Rock-

How to Rack Gear

When you're racking gear, be organized. There are a couple of logical variations on racking.

One method calls for you to look at the route and determine what to take for protection (gear, pro, or pieces). Then organize gear in the order that it will be needed. The frontmost piece of gear on the front gear loop should be the first piece you'll use. Place the anticipated second piece of gear behind the first and continue in this fashion until the gear loop is full. Then fill the other loops in the same way, from front to back.

Another handy way to rack is to organize gear on the loops according to its type and size. For example, place all your passive pro (Wallnuts and Rockcentrics) on one loop, with the smallest in front and working larger toward the back of the loop. On another gear loop, clip all the size 1 and 1.5 Friends. The next loop could hold all size 2 and 2.5 Friends, and so on.

Place the cams on your rack each on its own carabiner. Place no more than two or three wired nuts on each biner. Any more than that makes it difficult to sort out the correct size quickly. If over-the-shoulder slings (60 centimeter) are required, place two carabiners on each so they're ready for placement. Lastly, have a few quickdraws or "free" carabiners (three to five linked together like a chain) as you deem necessary.

However you rack your gear, make sure it's organized and remember where it is on the rack. An organized and well-remembered rack can save crucial time when you're fighting to place gear, leading to greater climbing enjoyment. By memorizing your rack arrangement, you can often reach and select the correct, intended piece without looking down to sift through assorted pro.

On straight-in cracks it's usually better to clip the smaller, less bulky pieces on the front loops to allow your legs more unencumbered movement. Clip larger, lower-hung pieces toward the rear of the harness where they're less likely to be in your way.

For dihedrals where one side of your body will scrape against the rock, clip as much gear as possible, especially large pieces, on the opposite side of the harness. This will lower the discomfort and the risk of bruising to your thighs. Racking on the side facing away from the wall will also keep your gear from scratching the rock, which sometimes severely scars and causes untimely erosion to dihedral walls. For evidence of such scarring, just take a look at the popular dihedrals in Indian Creek. Here, oblivious climbers' racked gear has gouged light-colored swaths through the sandstone's natural dark patina running bottom to top of certain pitches. It's a clear testament to human interference, as bold as the classic KILROY WAS HERE.

If you're racking for a narrow to midsize chimney, locate your gear away from the back of your harness to avoid pain and gear snags.

Organize the rack on the loops according to type and size of gear.

Rack smaller, less cumbersome cams on the front gear loops and larger, bulkier cams toward the back.

centrics, and one set of Tech Friends. Packed thusly, you could climb a variety of the Tower's 5.9s and 5.10s. More difficult routes may require a second set of Friends.

Rope

The various types of ropes were discussed in chapter 7, but we'd like to note here that when you're visiting a specific crag, take a close look at rope length versus route length. First, check the guidebook to see how long the pitches and rappels are. This will help you determine how many ropes to take, and of what lengths.

If no route on your would-be tick list is longer than 35 meters, then one 70-meter rope will be long enough for both ends to be on the ground, while the middle runs through the anchor. If the pitches are 70 meters long, but none requires a rappel, then one 70-meter rope will probably be sufficient, too (bi-pattern is best for this situation). But if a pitch is 70 meters long and requires you to rap back down the route descending the entire 70 meters nonstop, then two 70-meter ropes will be mandatory.

Other Staples

Other equipment to bring includes shoes, harness, daisy chain, chalk bag, tape, water and food, helmet if desired, and anything else that you routinely use during a day at the crags. See "Additional Hardware and Necessities" in chapter 7 for more information about these items.

Remember to take the all-American apple pie to enjoy after climbing.

9

Leading

Lead climbing is deeply rewarding. Successfully leading a pitch that is close to your ability level creates a sense of accomplishment exceeding even the joy of a successful toprope adventure.

Leading takes confidence; it also builds confidence. Like a muscle that becomes stronger with use, confidence is replenished at a rate greater than its expenditure, if you exercise it regularly.

Belaying a Leader

Belaying a leader on a crack climb is a good introduction to leading itself. The word *belay* has nautical origins; it refers to tying a marine line to a post or a hitch. For climbing purposes, *to belay* refers to holding the rope to keep a climber safe from falling. This book assumes that you understand the overall concept of belaying. Belaying a lead climber is a more strenuous challenge than belaying a person on toprope, and belaying a crack climber can be more stressful still. But the experience of belaying a leader on a crack will give you a better understanding of what leading is all about.

When you're belaying from a standing position on flat ground, you may or may not be clipped in to an anchor. It's not always necessary to set up an anchor, especially if the landing is flat and there's nowhere for the belayer to go but up. That stated, the farther you're pulled up during a lead falling episode, the lower the leader will sail. A leader who

Crack climbing **Comes the Dervish (E3 5C) is fun on slippery Welsh slate.**

greatly outweighs you may decide it's wise to set up an anchor to hold you to the ground. This can be done by tying you to a tree or huge rock, clipping in to belay bolts if they're available, or by installing gear into the crack or cracks. If there's any danger that you'll be pulled from a precarious perch, or on any multipitch route, you should always be securely anchored on belay.

In addition, it's often wise to anchor the belay system itself. This will alleviate strain on your body by sending the pull from a lead fall onto the belay system directly. You should still be clipped into the belay device in most cases, but your position can be arranged so that the climber's weight won't be loaded onto you, but onto the anchored device.

When a leader is about to embark on a pitch, strongly consider setting an upward directional belay. This directional piece (or pieces) is set primarily to hold an upward pull, most likely as part of the belay anchor. When the leader falls above a piece of protection, above the anchor, the rope is pulled up toward the first piece of lead gear, and so is the belay system. As belayer, you'll appreciate the chance for the upward directional and the system to take the shock of the leader's falling weight.

The leader's first pro should take an upward directional, too, for safety. See "Special Placements and Considerations" in chapter 7.

Belaying a leader who is placing gear can be a daunting task. Sometimes the leader will attempt to place pro, but will drop it. Be ready to duck. Standing to the side, out of the path of any falling gear or rock that the leader peels off, is sound advice in many cases. Sometimes the leader will be too

Belaying a leader who is placing gear on a crack climb can be a daunting task that requires full attention. Looking up all the time is painful, so most belayers watch the rope for clues as to the leader's progress.

pumped to place the gear well and can no longer hold on to the jams, but can't clip the manqué gear, either. Be ready to catch. If a leader is run out too far from the last piece, you may need to be unanchored, which will give you the freedom to run or jump from the belay stance as you work to keep the leader from hitting the ground.

Following a Leader

Following a leader is a good way to learn not only basic crack climbing techniques but also solid gear placement. A real-world gear-placement instructor is always going to be better than one on paper, disk, or screen. There's nothing like the real thing, whether it's a professional guide or a credible mentor who's a friend and climbing partner. Of course, be sure to assess his or her qualifications.

Following a leader who has placed bomber gear at safe intervals is a great learning opportunity. As follower, you'll typically clean the route, removing everything the leader placed. Before you take out a piece, though, examine both the type of gear and the spot in the crack where it was positioned. Was it a nut seated in a constriction, or was it a cam placed in a parallel-sided crack? How much rock surface contact was there, and where did the gear touch the rock? Would it have protected a fall from the direction that the leader would have traveled? In some cases, especially when evaluating the first piece, it's important to ask: Would this gear have held if it had taken an upward pull from the leader falling on the piece above it? Was it placed where you might prefer to jam instead? Was there an alternative placement spot that would have worked as well or better? The more attention you pay to such details, the more you can learn from

The Pitfalls of Belaying

Sometimes it takes nearly as much bravery to belay as it does to climb. Take the layered slate quarry in North Wales, near Llanberis (pronounced *clan-bear-iss*) in Gwynedd (Gwineth). The Dinorwig quarry consists of Cambrian, dolphin-skin-slick slate. At its deepest point it has numerous human-made terraces approximately 8 feet wide separating each successive layer. Here climbers flake out their rope and gear up for a slicker-than-snot rock adventure.

The good thing about climbing a sparsely protected route is that the required rack is very, very light. On one famous John Redhead X-rated route, *Pull My Daisy*, aspiring leaders would be thrilled to discover a third protection point in the 80 or so feet of the pitch, but it's not there. So how *do* you climb this route? Let's see.

To start, you—as leader—ascend a few meters above a small cam or wire protecting the opening moves, then climb high above to a rusty old pipe that was part of the cleaving mechanism left in place by slate quarrymen. You must tie off the protruding 2-foot pipe with webbing and then proceed high above it, most likely to the top of the terrace, with no additional gear. As the action continues, the pipe becomes a distant piece, directly below and centered between your legs.

But here's the thing about this quarry. If you were to fall here—

unlikely but certainly possible—you could become impaled on the pipe. Ouch! Failing that gruesome fate, you could also be racked on the pipe—before it rips from the wall, that is. How to

(continued on page 122)

This belayer may need to jump off the edge behind him into the abyss of this multileveled slate quarry in North Wales in a last-ditch effort to save a falling leader from a grounder. **Pull My Daisy (E2 5C), near Llanberis.**

(continued from page 121)
save you from a grounder? Well, to accomplish that, your teary and wet belayer would need to jump from the edge of the terrace into the void below. You and your belayer would both sail downward, pinning your hopes on the first piece of gear. It's doubtful that the belayer could jump quickly enough to completely stop you from hitting the ledge, but if the gear holds—and after you've bounced off the terrace—the two of you could find yourselves hanging like clackers high above the floor of the pit.

A rating of *X* means that death or serious injury may occur. In the situation described above, however, it could be proposed that the X rating really refers to the profanity expelled during a fall of such duration!

After climbing at the quarry, you can take a nice dip into the nearby lake and swim with the eels . . . but that's another story.

After basic crack climbing techniques are learned, following a leader and cleaning gear is an opportunity to learn about placements.

appraising the gear placements of an experienced leader.

Was the gear placed at a well-thought-out interval so that a lead fall from any position before the lower piece would have been stopped safely? A leader will fall more than twice as far as the last piece of gear is below him or her. In other words, if the knot at the leader's harness is 10 feet above the last gear and the leader falls from that position, then the length of the fall will be more than 20 feet. You need to figure 20 feet for the fall itself, extra footage to compensate for rope stretch, and more still if there was slack in the rope at the time of the fall.

These are just some of the many points to consider before jumping on the sharp end of the rope and leading a crack.

Leading

Leading requires knowledge and preparation. In particular, a thorough understanding of gear usage is critical to a safe lead climbing experience. And of course, no book can provide as well rounded a picture of gear placement as the real world can. We recommend employing a professional guide or climbing with a credible mentor. The decision to lead a route should be taken very seriously. A realistic self-evaluation of your comfort and competency level is crucial for safety.

Placing gear on lead is strenuous and makes a route effectively much more difficult than it would be on toprope or even on pre-placed gear or bolts.

***A leader targets a Friend placement. Proper placement requires comprehension
and accurate evaluation.*** KLAUS FENGLER/RED CHILI

Leading

To Lead or Not to Lead?

> *To be, or not to be: that is the question:*
> *Whether 'tis nobler in the mind to suffer*
> *The slings and arrows of outrageous fortune,*
> *Or to take arms against a sea of troubles,*
> *And by opposing end them?*
>
> —WILLIAM SHAKESPEARE,
> *HAMLET* (ACT III, SCENE I)

Leading requires sustained holding power and control over emotions. Gear placement should be logical and structurally sound, not a panic-mode tossing of stuff at a crack and hoping something will stick!

Confidence, accurate self-assessment, fluency with gear—all are critical to a happy journey up a crack, but they're not enough. You must also be able to properly calculate the total effect of external variables. For example, a route blazing in the sun on a hot day may make a fine climb—but perhaps one better left until the sun leaves and the rock cools. Blinding rays and sweat pouring from the skin may cause an unnecessary challenge.

Excessive wind, too, can wreak havoc with your balance, body temperature, and communication with the belayer. Wind can cause the rope to become ensnared on vegetation or rock features. It can blow a loose end or a loop out of reach, where it may become caught on a flake or a limb. Gale-force wind . . . not so good.

Hail hurts. Looking up for jams and gear placements only to have your eyes battered by ice pellets and swollen shut is just not good. Hail can make the crack icy or wet. Climbing during a hailstorm is contraindicated.

Lightning is another real danger. Avoid being on a wall during a lightning storm whenever possible.

After a rain it may be best to wait until the crack dries out before attempting to climb it. Some rock, especially sandstone, is weaker when moisture has permeated its pores and may not hold gear as well as it would if it were dry. Fog should be counted with other precipitation as a potential rock-weakening agent. Sandstone may act like a sponge, soaking moisture from the air during a fog event. Beside the strength issue, a crack running wet with slime does not provide good friction for climbing.

Rock quality is a huge consideration when leading and placing gear. No matter how textbook-perfect a placement may look, gear can rip from the wall along with crumbles or chunks of rock if the rock is friable. You must be able to distinguish solid rock from soft, weak rock, and to differentiate secure flakes from those that can flex or break. Dirty, scaly, lichen-covered rock or rock with ball bearings on its surface should be highly suspect.

Bailing Off

Reasons to Bail Off

> *A fool too late bewares when all the peril is past.*
>
> —QUEEN ELIZABETH I

Truth be told, there are probably more justifiable reasons to bail off a route than there is rationale for climbing it in the first place. What follows is a Top Ten list of indicators that retreat rather than charge may be the preferred stratagem.

10. Rational or irrational fear.
9. Insufficient skill level.
8. Exhaustion or injury.
7. Weather dangers or poor weather conditions.
6. Risk assessment of environmental danger or friable rock.
5. Not enough rope.
4. Improper gear selection, or not enough of it.
3. Strategic conservation of energy for a better attempt later.
2. My damn shoes are no good.

And the number 1 reason to bail off:
"I just don't like this stupid route!"

Placing gear on lead is strenuous and makes a route much more difficult than it would be on toprope or on pre-placed gear or bolts. **Scarface (5.11), Indian Creek.** BRIAN BAILEY

The Fog

Once upon a time, two experienced climbers (who shall go unnamed) went to the desert to do the first and second ascent of a new route. It was sure to be a very difficult grade. The mood was serious, yet filled with an air of adventure.

When morning came, dawn did not break. No red rays, no gleaming beams casting hues on cliff or cloud. A low-lying fog had rolled in, filling the canyons with deepening mist. It came in the form of a white serpent crawling between the canyons' walls, like ghostly blood coursing through a vein. One of the pair quoted Merlin's line from *Excalibur*: "Can't you see all around you, the dragon's breath?" Was it merely a dream, or had the dragon awoken?

Lost in a cloud, the climbers got racked and ready for battle with the thin crack that seemed to slither up the wall and vanish into the cloud. They would not be deterred by vapors exhaled from a giant, winged lizard. Fools!

Given the severe difficulty of the task at hand and the lack of any other route appropriate for a warm-up, the climbers decided they would each make an initial ascent of the crack, hanging to rest or lowering off before becoming too pumped. Then they would pull the rope and the gear and try for a redpoint-style FFA.

The first climber left the ground, placing gear close together in a nod to the rock's soft quality. The belayer, seeing that the rope might become entangled in a small dead bush, moved to kick the wooden skeleton from the cliff base and send it down the steeply angled talus. Then she stopped before making contact; she felt sure that the mist had somehow told her to leave this bush's corpse intact, to decay in its own due time.

The leader was making easy progress, sewing the crack tight with gear and rope. Up the crack 50 feet into the fog he went until at last his voice drifted down to the belayer: "Take." Hoping to stop before fatigue set in, he intended to lower from that point, having placed a solid cam at waist height. This protection wasn't far above all the other textbook-perfect placements, in a tightly stitched progression. The belayer pulled in as much rope as possible and leaned backward, suspended over the rim of the talus. Up above, the leader sat back on the rope to be taken. In the same instant, the belayer fell, head-first and faceup, into the talus. It was as if the lifeline had been cut and the leader and belayer were no longer attached.

The belayer heard the striking of rocks upon rocks, the jingling of gear, and the dull *thud* of a body landing like a watermelon hitting the floor.

A chill of dread shivered up the belayer's spine. Her first thoughts were of the hand on the rope. Had she inadvertently let go? No. Her hand still tightly grasped the rope. Struggling upright to see the rock wall, the belayer looked up through her skyward legs. She could see the crack, but no climber. Only the first piece of gear remained in the crack, looming above a pile of gear and rope at the route's base.

A moment of confusion was accompanied by the rustling of another talus-bound body. "Check my head! Check my head!" the breathless voice from the upside-down leader pleaded. Finding the leader heels-over-head, a yard away, with his skull resting on a large pointed rock, the belayer braced for the worst and reached out. No blood, no brains exposed . . . keep looking! The only evidence of injury from the fall was a shallow inch-long scratch on the back of the leader's head. Not a break, sprain, or bruise was apparent. How could this be?

Between the skull and the pointed rock lay the smithereens of the old dead bush—the same bush that the belayer hadn't kicked away. The splintering of its twigs and branches had completely buffered the blow to the climber's head. Could the corpse bush have had a destiny to fulfill? Are humans the only entities upon which fate acts?

The leader and belayer looked up at the crack. All but the first piece of protection had ripped. And everywhere that the gear had been, cantaloupe- and croissant-shaped chunks of rock had exploded from the wall as well. The gear hadn't failed—the rock had.

Seconds later, after realizing that he was virtually uninjured, the leader leapt to his feet and announced that he had a Bosch drill in the car; he intended to run right down (an extremely loose and steep mile) and grab it. He would then run right back up, bolt the route, and send it that day despite everything that had just happened.

The belayer suspected that the 50-foot pile-drive the leader had just made into the ground may have affected his assessment abilities and persuaded him to wait a moment before his jaunt to the car. Reluctantly, he untied, took off his shoes, and sat down to relax. Meanwhile, the belayer packed the gear away. A few minutes later the leader gave in. The pair headed down the talus, calling it a day. The leader's pace slowed with every step, but he did make it to the car with only minor bodily support from the belayer. In the end, there were no broken bones, just a very sore lower back from the impact and a tiny scratch on the head.

The bush, of course, was not so lucky.

*Even good desert sandstone on **Sacred Cow** (5.12d) is soft rock, difficult to trust.* BRIAN BAILEY

How to Bail Off

There are several common means of retreat from a crack. Let's look briefly at a few of them.

RAP OR LOWER OFF

One way to bail from a crack is to set an anchor and rappel or lower off, abandoning the ascent completely. This book assumes that you're proficient at setting anchors. If not, consult a manual such as *Climbing Anchors* by John Long and Bob Gaines.

It's crucial to properly gauge the amount of rope available for lowering or rapping. If the belayer isn't already tied in to the other end of the rope, tie a knot with at least 8 inches of tail at the end of the rope (or the rope should be tied properly through the belayer's harness before lowering the leader). If you incorrectly calculate the rope length needed to return safely to the belay, you could end up stranded on the end of the line. Such a predicament may require you to set another anchor, clip directly into the anchor via locking carabiner(s) on a sling to the harness's tie-in loop or belay loop, untie the rope from the harness and pull it down through the previous anchor, catch the end, tie back in, ensure that the rope is clipped through the new, lower anchor, make sure your belayer has you back on tight belay or that the rappel is correctly set up, unclip the sling connecting your harness to the anchor, lean back on the rope, and continue to rap or lower down. Did that sound like a run-on sentence? Well, it certainly feels like a run-on process when it must actually be performed!

On multipitch routes you must take care to find the balance between placing enough gear in the first rappel anchor and also conserving enough gear on the rack to set additional rap anchors lower on the route if necessary.

The logical consequence of this bailing method? Plan a trip to the gear shop to replenish all the forfeited pro on your rack.

DOWN-AID

Often a less expensive way to bail is to down-aid or downclimb. In down-aiding you may clip slings (possibly over-the-shoulder length) for use as steps, while clipping or threading additional slings through the harness tie-in point or belay loop to keep you stationary while you remove gear above. Reach down to clip the step-sling into the lower piece, place your foot in the sling, stand on it, slink down, and clip in to the piece at the waist. Then reach back up, unclip the rope from the higher piece, remove the pro, and place it on your gear rack. You can only do this if the pro has been placed close together, or if you place intermediate pieces for use on your descent.

DOWNCLIMB

On lead a downclimb is similar to a lead ascent, but in reverse. Climb down to a spot where the top piece of gear in the crack is within reach from your stance. Unclip the rope, remove the gear, climb down to the next piece, and repeat. As easy as this may sound, most people find downclimbing more difficult and possibly scarier than upclimbing. Odd, because gravity helps a climber move down!

NEW LEADER

Sometimes the leader wishes to bail from the lead and another person in the climbing party is willing to take over. This scenario is simple as long as the leader has enough rope to get back to the belayer. (We repeat: *as long as the leader has enough rope to get back to the belayer.*) The belayer should tie a knot in the end of the rope before lowering the retreating leader if there's any doubt as to whether the leader will make it back to the belay. The leader can be lowered to the ground (or to the belay stance on a multipitch route) and swap ends with the next batter up. Be absolutely sure, in the multipitch situation, that both climbers are clipped in to the anchor independently with slings before untying from the rope. The ground may be a long way off, but the sudden stop at the end is sure to spoil the rest of your life. The new leader can pull the rope down through the gear to get a more comprehensive leading experience, or may decide to climb with the rope in situ (on toprope) until reaching the point where he or she passes the top piece of protection and truly takes over the lead.

It's crucial to correctly gauge the amount of rope needed for a rappel. If there's any chance that the rope won't reach the ground, tie a knot in the end for safety.

AID

Despite Todd Skinner's exhortation, "Aid isn't climbing!" sometimes, instead of retreating downward, you may decide to switch to aid climbing as a way to ascend to the end of the pitch. This happens when the leader is physically or mentally tired, or the route is too difficult to free climb. If you're not free climbing, then you're aiding. It is just that simple.

The main purpose of using aid as a way to bail is to get to the end of the pitch; there, a fixed anchor can provide a safe descent or regrouping point. On a multipitch route an anchor may provide a stopping point where the climbing team can switch leaders. There are many versions of weighting gear in order to ascend by aid. Fat books have been written about aid and this isn't one of them, but we'll briefly mention a couple of common ways to use aid for bailing off.

Aiding might include clipping in to gear and sitting on it for a rest, then continuing in free-climbing fashion until another rest is required after placing higher gear. Or you could stand in a sling, place higher gear, grab the newly placed gear or biner, pull up—asking the belayer to "take"—and repeat as often as necessary. This process requires the belayer to take your weight when you have pro at your waist, and then quickly provide slack when you're pulling on gear to move higher. As leader, you can clip in at each protection placement to take some of the load off your belayer. As usual, a good and patient belayer is indispensable.

ROUTES

Occasionally, the best or only way to continue your ascent is to traverse to another route that's easier, safer, or in some way better. This may also allow you to reach another anchor, or to find a spot to set an anchor for bailing. A hanging climber might also swing (pendulum) over to another route, crack, or anchor.

Warning: There are a lot of ways to mess up the bailing process, with serious consequences. If you'd like to learn more, any number of articles and books have been devoted to safety topics and/or the misadventures related to bailing off. This book is not designed to cover the multitude of potential scenarios and flubs.

Styles of Ascent

Much that once was is lost, for none now live who remember it.

—GALADRIEL,
FROM *LORD OF THE RINGS* BY J. R. R. TOLKIEN

There are many styles of ascent, and it's important to know the differences among them. Most climbers take a certain pride in knowing they have climbed specific routes on-sight, flash, or redpoint. Aid climbing uses gear for resting and ascent. If you know you don't have sufficient skill or stamina for a route, you might want to aid climb it. Many multipitch routes have points of aid or entire aid pitches. Free climbing uses only the body for ascent; gear is used solely for protection in case of a fall. We possess a strong preference for free climbing and the particular way it tests the mind, spirit, and body.

Sport climbs may have quickdraws fixed on the bolt hangers or not, and the style of ascent is considered the same either way. The main idea behind sport climbing is to focus on movement rather than protection. Trad (traditional) routes, however, do not follow this rule—here, placing the gear is integral to the difficulty of the climbing. Routes that require nuts or cams for protection are much more taxing because you must stay on each jam or hold longer to find the proper piece on your rack, and then place the protection well. A good way to experience the differences in difficulty among styles of ascent is to toprope a crack, and then lead the same crack placing pro from the ground up. To up the ante, try leading the route first, placing gear on lead; afterward, toprope the same route for comparison.

The commonly acknowledged styles of ascent are as follows:

An **on-sight solo** is generally taken to mean an ascent with no prior knowledge of the route, no

*Steve Petro on-sight soloing England's **Goliath** (E4 6A). Off-widths may require special outfits . . . or did he just come from his job at Wiener on a Stick in the mall?*

Toproping is a safe way to learn the intricacies of climbing off-width cracks on soft desert towers. Here, Linda Givler makes her way up Owl Rock in Arches National Park.

PART III: HITTING THE CRAGS

pro, and no rope. That is, a fall will almost certainly result in death or hospitalization. This is not recommended.

Yeah, well, I guess he had it coming.
—THE SCHOFIELD KID, UNFORGIVEN

We all got it coming, kid.
—RESPONSE FROM WILL MUNNY

On-sight refers to a leader climbing a route for the first time without falling, having seen no one else on the route and using no beta (tips on how to do moves, where to find holds, or the like) from friends or anyone else. This is the probably most difficult style of roped, free ascent and could be considered the purest form of ascent after the on-sight solo.

To **flash** is to climb the route for the first time without falling, but this time with beta. The word *beta* came to climbing from those old-style videocassettes, Betamax, a formerly popular medium for watching films. In this case, getting beta means previewing a route and moves before climbing it. You might obtain beta by talking to or by watching another climber on the same route before the flash attempt.

A **redpoint** ascent refers to climbing the route without falling, but not on your first attempt; you've fallen on at least one previous try. If you're working a project for days or weeks, and then climb the route without falling, this is also a redpoint. Again, on sport climbs the quickdraws can be fixed. Trad climbs, on the other hand, must be stripped of protection before subsequent attempts. Every attempt must be done carrying pro up the climb and placing it on lead for a valid redpoint of a crack climb or trad route.

The term *redpoint* is derived from the German word *rotpunkt*, coined in the mid-1970s by the climbing superhero Kurt Albert, who lives and climbs in the Frankenjura. He pioneered much of the free climbing in the Frankenjura and some of the area's most famous and difficult routes. Once

he was able to free climb a route that had previously contained points of aid, he would put a red dot of paint at the base of the route. Differentiating aid and free climbing in this way probably led to the development of sport climbing a decade later. Some say that hard sport climbing started in France in the 1980s, with Germany a close second.

Pinkpoint is an obscure term used to describe an ascent with fixed gear or quickdraws. Here, the gear has been left in place after an ascent to make subsequent attempts easier and provide the leader with a greater likelihood of success. This term was popularly used in the late 1980s and early 1990s when sport climbing was in its infancy in the United States. Now it's hardly ever heard; sport climbers tend to refer to all pinkpoints and redpoints as simply redpoints—an unfortunate loss of a valuable word. Climbing cracks pinkpoint-style displays a lack of commitment since placing gear is integral to the difficulty of climbing cracks. However, a first free ascent of a crack may be pinkpointed. Of course, another climber may up the ante by on-sighting, flashing, or truly redpointing this same route to claim a superior style of ascent.

A **yo-yo** is an ascent where, upon falling, you lower to the ground but leave your rope through the protection—whether that be nuts, cams, or quickdraws—ready for the next attempt. In essence, you'll be on toprope until you pass the highest piece of protection from your previous attempt. As a result, the next attempt is not as difficult as it would have been if you'd pulled the rope and gear for another redpoint attempt. Well, we climbers do what we do. On the last day of a trip a long way from home, you may well choose to settle for something less than a redpoint.

Hangdog is a crusty old term applied to a person who falls or rests on the rope but requests to be held without being lowered. Hanging and rehearsing moves is commonly called "working" or "dogging" a route. The belayer will hold you steady at the high point so you can inspect the rock for foot- and fingerholds. Through such inspection, and often by rehearsing moves, you hope to find a bet-

A toprope ascent gives this climber a chance to concentrate on finger jams with one hand thumbs-up, the other thumbs-down.

PART III: HITTING THE CRAGS

ter way to ascend the route than during previous attempts. If you continue to the top of the pitch after resting on gear, you must be honest and not claim to have "done" the climb. This is not an on-sight, flash, or redpoint. It's an attempt and nothing more.

What's the secret to success? There's nothing secret about the concept of hard work!

A **siege** is a desperate attempt by a team of climbers to ascend a pitch. When one climber falls or becomes tired and lowers to the bottom, the others climb up with the protection and rope left in yo-yo-style. The difference here is that climbers take turns tag-teaming the pitch. This is not an ascent that you'd brag about, but it is a way to get the rope to the top of the climb.

Toproping means that a rope is protecting you from above. There are a couple of ways to create a TR. The belayer may sit at the top of the pitch, pulling rope up as you approach. Or you can use a rope that runs through an anchor at the top of the route with both ends reaching the bottom of the route—one end for you the climber, the other for the belayer. A rope set in this fashion is sometimes called a slingshot. Although you may free climb the route by ascending using only body parts and without falls, it's not an on-sight or flash; it's a toprope ascent. Toproping provides a safer and less strenu-ous way to check out a route than leading.

Although hanging from the end of the rope can't always be avoided, the greatest sense of accomplishment in rock climbing is ascending a pitch bottom-to-top without falling or hanging. A great partner, great route, great location, or great *whatever* each contributes to feeling great about rock climbing . . . yet there's no comparison to achieving a route that pushes your personal limits.

Conclusion

There is no substitute for real-life experience. Still, learning via a how-to book can serve as both an introduction and an overview to a very large subject.

Reading about crack climbing exposes you to concepts and techniques that you might otherwise encounter only after years of climbing experience. It's a kind of shortcut along the learning curve, anticipating many of your questions.

We hope this instructional book will help you accomplish everything you want to do, as well as warning you about some common obstacles.

Above all, though, we hope we've prepared you to have lots of fun in the cracks. A journey of 1,000 miles—or 1,000 vertical feet—begins with a single step.

Happy Journey,
Lisa and Steve

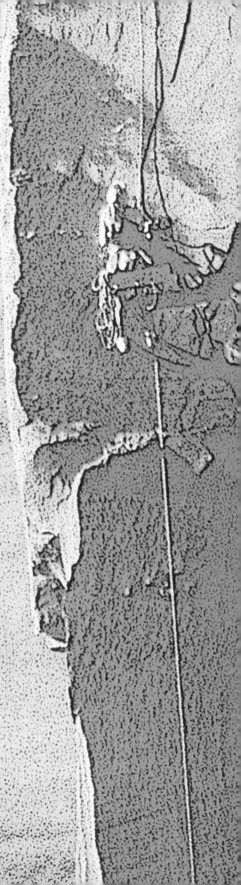

Have I Left the Eagle
to Soar in Freedom

The time will soon be here when my grandchild
*   will long for the cry of a loon,*
*   the flash of a salmon,*
*   the whisper of spruce needles,*
*   or the screech of an eagle.*
But he will not make friends
*   with any of these creatures*
*   and when his heart aches with longing*
*   he will curse me.*
Have I done all to keep the air fresh?
Have I cared enough about the water?
Have I left the eagle to soar in freedom?
Have I done everything I could to earn
*   my grandchild's fondness?*
                      —CHIEF DAN GEORGE
            FROM *THE BEST OF CHIEF DAN GEORGE*

Glossary of Crack Climbing Terms

Aid   Weighting gear in order to navigate on rock.

Anchor   A point or grouping of points set to protect the belay.

Arête   An outside corner of rock.

Bail   To back off or in some way abort an ascent.

Belay   Holding the rope to protect the climber; used as both noun and verb.

Beta   Sharing of information about a route or its moves by audio, visual, written, or other means.

Boink   A process in which the climber grasps the rope and pulls the body up as the belayer pulls against the fallen leader with all his or her weight.

Box   A U-shaped formation, ordinarily with two dihedrals in the back of the recess.

Cam   An active fall protection device having spring-loaded, logarithmic-spiraled lobes set at a constant 13.75 degrees; used as both noun and verb.

Carabiner   Snap link, biner.

Chalk   Magnesium carbonate, gymnastics chalk.

Chimney   A crack in a rock, wide enough to allow passage for the whole body.

Chock   A block, rock, or wedge inside a crack, used as fall protection.

Clean   (1) An ascent with no falls or hangs, performed without touching the gear as a means of moving higher; a *clean* ascent. (2) To remove gear from a route.

Dihedral   An inside corner of rock with two faces.

Directional   A piece of gear that is placed to direct the path of the rope.

Double ropes   A two-rope system often used to avoid rope drag. One rope clips pieces on the climber's left, and a different-colored rope clips pieces on the right.

Dynamic elongation   Rope stretch.

Flakes   Thin exfoliates or shards of rock that are separated but still attached to the wall, forming holds or crevices that can be climbed or used for gear placement.

Flappers   Flaps of skin ripped loose, exposing bloody underlayers.

Flash   An ascent of a route for the first time, without falling, but having beta.

Follow   To climb second after a leader while belayed on toprope, often cleaning the pitch.

Gaston   To pull sideways, as in prying open an elevator door.

Good style   A free lead ascent with no falls, no hangs, accomplished without weighting gear.

Grade   Difficulty rating of a climb. The Yosemite Decimal System (YDS) is used in the United States; other rating systems are used around the globe.

Hangdog   Hanging on the rope to rest before continuing on a pitch; used as both noun and verb.

Hex   A six-sided nut with two ends most appropriately slung on Dyneema.

Inward flare   A crack that opens wider as it recedes into the formation.

Jam   Fitting hands, fingers, legs, feet, head, whole body, or a combination into a rock crevice; used as both noun and verb.

Lead   Going first, dragging the rope up, and protecting the route as upward progression is made; used as both noun and verb.

Lieback This creates opposing pressure between the fingers and the feet.

Multipitch A route with more than one pitch in succession.

Nut A passive aluminum or brass wedge typically slung on wire cable.

Off-width The name given to cracks that are larger than a fist but smaller than a torso.

On-sight The free ascent of a route on the first attempt without falling, with no prior knowledge of the route of any kind; used as both noun and verb.

On-sight solo A free ascent with no prior knowledge of the route, no pro, and no rope.

Outward flare A crack that becomes wider as it approaches the surface.

Pinkpoint A mostly obscure term for a clean, free ascent when the gear or quickdraws are fixed; used as both noun and verb.

Pitch The span between the belay and the anchor.

Pod A circular or elliptical undulation or divot in a crack.

Protection (pro) Gear or piece used to protect.

Pump Lactic acid burn and cramping (usually in the forearm) from sustained muscular contraction.

Rand The external rubber sidewall of the shoe.

Redpoint A free ascent of a route without falling, but not during the on-sight or flash attempt; used as both noun and verb.

Rope drag Friction created when the rope changes angles or rubs across a rough surface.

Roof A horizontal or overhanging section of rock that juts out or covers a cavity.

Rugosite A rough surface feature.

Scum A friction smear against the rock performed with a body part other than hands or feet.

Shake Dropping hands and shaking arms for circulation and recovery.

Shuffle Moving hands without crossing over, so that the top hand stays on top and bottom hand stays on bottom, usually with thumbs oriented toward each other.

Siege A team of climbers taking turns on a pitch, yo-yo-style, to move the rope higher.

Slab A low-angled sheet of rock.

Sling A loop of webbing.

Slingshot A toprope that runs through an anchor at the top of the route with both ends reaching the bottom of the route, one end for the climber, one for the belayer.

Splitter An even-sided crack running up the middle of a face, climbed straight in.

Stem Forming an X with the appendages and pressing outward against the rock to hold a suspended position; used as both noun and verb.

Take A command from the climber, asking the belayer to catch or hold the climber with the rope.

Toprope (TR) A rope protecting the climber from above; used as both noun and verb.

Undercling A way of holding or a hold on a rock that is grasped from underneath and utilized with palms facing upward or facing the climber; used as both noun and verb.

Undulate To move or appear to move in a wave-like manner.

Upward directional Gear set to hold an upward pull.

V-slot A constriction in which the rock necks down to form a V.

Vector A force defined by both magnitude and direction.

Working Rehearsing moves to find a better way to ascend the route than during previous attempts, often with the intention to redpoint.

Yo-yo An ascent where, upon falling, the climber lowers to the ground but leaves the rope through the protection for the next attempt; used as both noun and verb.

Zipper The unintentional high-speed ripping of multiple pieces of gear from a crack during a fall, sometimes resulting in a grounder.

About the Authors

Lisa Gnade

Rock climbing is more than an activity or a sport for Lisa; it's her way of life, and it's been her primary focus for more than twenty years. She began climbing during her years as a student at Flagstaff's Northern Arizona University in order to fulfill a required credit in physical education. It was an unplanned but gratifying turning point in her life, and it sent any pursuit of nine-to-five far astray.

Lisa has climbed dozens of 5.13 crack and sport routes across the globe. Her favorite climbing areas include Indian Creek, where she became known as the first woman in the world to consistently climb 5.13 cracks by completing both FFAs and repeats of established lines; Germany's Frankenjura, where she put up the hardest FFA by a woman to that date; and Kalymnos, Arkansas sandstone, Paradise Forks, Arco, and Mallorca, to name a few.

Now working as importer and distributor, sales manager, and sales representative for DMM and Wild Country climbing equipment and Red Chili climbing shoes, she finds herself with even greater appreciation for time on the rock. Her companion in both work and leisure is husband and fellow climbing enthusiast Steve Petro. When not climbing or working, Lisa can be found resort skiing in the Wasatch, reading foreign language and history textbooks, or spending time with her furry children, the cats. She lives in Sandy, Utah.

Steve Petro

Steve was born in Toronto, son of immigrant parents fleeing communism in Hungary. He was raised in Los Angeles, where in 1971 he proudly passed the test to become a US citizen. He later worked in the Wyoming oil fields before moving to Utah.

Rock climbing has been Steve's main athletic interest for the last thirty years. He is renowned for his many first ascents in Utah's Canyonlands and various locations in Wyoming. After climbing extensively throughout the United States and Europe, he lists among favorite climbing areas Indian Creek, American Fork, the Frankenjura, Kalymnos, Arkansas sandstone, Spanish limestone, and of course his old stomping ground, Fremont Canyon in Wyoming. Steve supports his climbing lifestyle by working as CEO of Excalibur, an importer of DMM and Wild Country climbing hardware and Red Chili shoes. When not climbing or working, Steve enjoys snowboarding, traveling, and reading books about current affairs, history, and myths.

Some of his most notable achievements include an FFA of the 1,800-foot route *Wind and Sand and Stars* (5.12c) in Zion National Park with Jeff Lowe and Lisa Gnade, and the FFA of the East Face of Cloud Peak via the 900-foot route *Shimmering Abstraction* (5.11) in the Bighorn Mountains (with Arno Ilgner). He was the first person to free climb 5.12 in the Tetons, on Mount Moran. In 1987 Steve accomplished the FFA of *Fiddler on the Roof*, Wyoming's premier roof crack and a route that went unrepeated until 2006. He lives in Sandy, Utah.

Point.
Click.
Send.

Climbing.com